Be Our

This letter was written by the Templeton Prize Winner for 1983, Alexander Solzhenitsyn, to the Revd Michael Bourdeaux who won the prize in 1984.

The Revd Michael Bourdeaux
Keston College
England

4 March 1984
Cavendish, Vermont

Dear Friend,

May I congratulate you most warmly on being awarded the Templeton Prize!

Everyone who knows your modest and selfless Christian commitment to doing good will be rejoicing now at this decision by the international jury of The Templeton Prize.

The award also serves to bring into sharp focus the terrible persecution of religion in Communist-ruled countries towards which your work is directed. One reason more for the world to ponder on this inhuman threat to itself.

One important element in your great task is to defend and help Russian Christians, who were the first to feel the force of godless persecution in the twentieth century. We salute you.

From my very soul I wish you a long life and all strength on the battlefield of Faith!

Yours
ALEXANDER SOLZHENITSYN

Be Our Voice

The Story of Michael Bourdeaux
and Keston College

Jenny Robertson

Darton Longman and Todd
London

First published in 1984 by
Darton, Longman and Todd Ltd
89 Lillie Road, London SW6 1UD

ISBN 0 232 51618 9

British Library Cataloguing in Publication Data

Robertson, Jenny
  Be our voice.
  1. Persecution—Communist countries
  2. Christianity—Communist countries
  I. Title
  272'.9   BR1608.C7
  ISBN 0–232–51618–9

KESTON BOOK NO. 23
A proportion of the royalties from the sale of this
book is going to Keston College. If you wish to make
a donation to Keston, please send it to:
Keston College, Heathfield Road, Keston, Kent BR2 6BA

Phototypeset by Input Typesetting Ltd, London SW19 8DR
Printed and bound in Great Britain by
Cox & Wyman, Reading

To my husband

Contents

1

'Tell the West'

All Western support, supplying information, demonstrations, prayer, helps us a great deal.

Georgi Vins

We want you to feel with us in our suffering and cry out when we cannot: 'Enough!'

Father Gheorghe Calciu

'Tell the West the story of my people's sufferings,' begged the young Baptist girl in Leningrad. She unfolded newspaper cuttings from the national press: a photograph of children, hands clasped in prayer, beneath a caption which proclaimed, 'These children have now been taken from their parents who taught them to do such vile things.'

'Our homes and meeting-places are razed to the ground by bulldozers,' the girl went on. 'You see, in many provincial towns the authorities refuse to register churches. So when believers meet for worship it's considered illegal.' She pointed to a photograph showing rubble where a church had stood, to another picture of a hall once used for worship which had been turned into a library.

The girl was called Aida Skripnikova. She worked as a laboratory assistant in Leningrad and went Sunday by Sunday to the crowded Baptist church near the tram terminus four or five miles out from the city. Here Sunday by Sunday boys on motor bikes would disturb the service by revving up their engines outside the building. Inside the church was standing room only, with everyone squashed together so closely in their bulky winter garments that it was difficult to blow your nose or wipe away a sneeze.

Occasionally a foreigner found the way to the crowded church and Aida often tried to get into conversation, fighting against the restraints imposed on her by church elders who forcibly held her back.

Aware of the church leadership's guarded remarks that of course there *were* difficulties, but, after all, the church was open, and well attended too, Aida would protest, 'But I want people to know that believers are put into prison for their faith and their children are removed into state institutions for years on end.'

Aida herself was already in quite serious trouble. Even in her teens she had written what was considered an 'anti-Soviet' letter to *Pravda*, protesting at the attack on the novelist Pasternak whose book, *Dr Zhivago*, had been banned. She wasn't a believing Christian then, though her parents had been. Her childhood had been lived out in war-torn Leningrad, against a background of suffering and hardship; even so, believing friends of the family met together in Aida's home to read the Bible and pray, at great personal risk. When Aida was still very small her father was shot for being a pacifist. In her late teens Aida herself started to grope her way towards God; and by the time she was twenty-one she had become a deeply convinced and fearless Christian, determined to share her faith even though it was forbidden.

Patiently enduring freezing winds in a sub-zero temperature, Aida stood on a street corner one New Year's Eve, offering postcards on which she had written New Year greetings, while the world about her bustled by, busy with party-time celebrations. Passers-by were laden with flowers, chocolates, champagne. Women carried string bags bulging with shopping for which they had stood in weary queues. Children, bundled in so many layers of clothing that they looked for all the world like baby seals, slithered over slippery pavements, their eyes bright with anticipation of party treats and balloons. Perhaps few people had time to notice the brown-eyed girl with her bundle of cards. If they did take one of the attractive postcards and noticed the words, 'Happy New Year 1962', they may have smiled, pleased, but if they glanced at the handwritten poem which followed they might well have experienced shock and fear, for in her poem Aida urged citizens of an atheistic state to stop and look for God.

2

'Our years fly past,' her poem began, appropriately enough, but it went on: 'What answer will you give your Creator? What awaits you, my friend, beyond the grave?'

What awaited Aida more immediately was arrest, a trial the following April in a Comrades' Court and years of slander in the press in articles with such lurid titles as 'Don't be a corpse among the living', 'In the meshes of religious fanatics', 'Obscurantist baseness' and 'Pirates from the prayer house'.

'Aida is fearless' was the opinion of many of her friends, but plainly they feared for her. To the article 'Don't be a corpse among the living' Aida wrote a challenging reply which, of course, wasn't published. It vividly highlights the problems faced by believers in a society which denies them freedom.

> Let us imagine that you and I have decided to compete against each other in a race. And suddenly you tie my legs together and rush towards the finishing post. 'Hurray! I've won!' you cry triumphantly. 'Untie my legs! Set me free! Then you'll see who'll win,' I'll say. 'Untie your legs? Set you free? But that would be an encroachment upon my freedom!' you answer.
>
> We would not agree if we were given complete freedom and you were forbidden to carry on anti-religious propaganda. We would be against this, firstly because it would be dishonest, secondly because when anti-religious propaganda is being carried on, it is easier for us to show up the hollowness of your arguments . . . It is therefore quite understandable that you are afraid of giving us freedom.[1]

The Comrades' Court ordered Aida to leave Leningrad and work on a building site, but it was in fact three years before they carried out this decision. Aida, however, gave up her job and left Leningrad in order to stay with her sister in Ukraine, gathering information about harassment and persecution there. But she was already being followed by the police. As she attempted to travel back to Leningrad a fleet of police cars blocked her way to the station. Luckily for Aida, just at that point, a tourist bus pulled up full of sightseers. The police cars disappeared in a flash and Aida seized the moment to find a country bus and work her way back to Leningrad by a roundabout route.

But she was now homeless and unemployed. Without a job she couldn't get a permit to live in Leningrad, but without an address she couldn't apply for a job. Eventually a Christian believer, an elderly woman, took pity on Aida. She was pitifully poor, living in a disused truck in railway sidings, but she took Aida in, and Aida managed to find a job in a factory where she worked for twelve hours a day putting tops on bottles.

It must have been an incredibly lonely time for Aida. Few people understood her. Local Christians, fearful for her, urged her to return to her studies. The elders and pastors were caught in a hopeless web of half-truths, under constant pressure from the authorities. No one seemed to share Aida's burning conviction that the plight of her persecuted fellow-believers should be publicized, that Christians should be given the freedom to publish and sell their own literature, that life should be lived without the daily dishonest compromise too many people seemed to consider inevitable. 'The society you will build will never be just, because you yourselves are unjust,' Aida had declared in her unpublished article. 'I am deeply convinced that where there is no truth, there can be no happiness either.'

With her tremendous enthusiasm for telling the truth, Aida's only hope seemed to be the occasional foreign visitor to the church, but even those who spoke Russian and had become familiar with the country found it almost incomprehensible, listening to careful official reports about church life, that the violation of basic human freedom Aida described really went on. Aida herself supposed that the so-called Christian West would give maximum coverage to her news and announce it in every headline; instead she herself was brought to trial, accused of harming her country.

'Our country could be the most beautiful in the world were there no persecution here,' Aida declared staunchly.

'Tell the West,' she had begged in 1962. But who would listen? The Soviet Union was still virtually a closed world. People in the West were afraid, confused, ill informed.

Christians were used to missionary work in the furthest corners of the globe, but missions to the Communist world were virtually unknown. Stalin had been dead for only nine years. Russian tanks in Budapest were a very recent memory. Student exchanges, it is true, were beginning to open up invaluable contacts for a small, though increasing number of people; but mostly it seemed that if you were interested in Russian you were, by definition, decidedly way-out, even perhaps a Communist! And the other Slavonic languages were (and are) hardly studied. The Orthodox Church, moreover, appeared hopelessly archaic and obscure to the Westerner. Besides, Western Christians in those days hardly conversed across denominational boundaries. Aida's voice seemed fated to die away unheard. Her brave gesture in snow-bound Leningrad on the eve of the 'Swinging Sixties' seemed a futile pebble flung at a fearsome giant.

Yet ten years later a book[2] was published about Aida which was later reprinted in paperback and translated into Spanish, German, Norwegian, Swedish and Finnish. The book made a striking impact on its readers who identified strongly with Aida and became aware that here was a real issue, not some academic exercise for the specialist, but something involving everyone who cares about human rights. Aida herself was in the forefront of producing *samizdat* (unofficial, self-published documents and literature) which has done so much to give colour, life and information to Christian literature in East and West, as well as having a profoundly enriching spiritual impact.

Indeed, twenty years since Aida desperately tried to 'tell the West', sacrificing her livelihood, security and freedom, the media here are now alerted at once as soon as a Christian is hounded to court, to prison or psychiatric ward. By no means every story reaches the West and, unfortunately, only those with what is considered 'topicality' seem to find their way into our newspapers or broadcasts, but the information is available. In fact, as these words were being written, the phone rang and in the course of conversation BBC Radio Scotland stated strongly how invaluable it is to have a totally reliable source of such information readily to hand.

What a different picture from the lonely girl in Leningrad

5

struggling to free herself from the restraining grasp of her own church elders in her efforts to inform the world about the plight of her fellow-believers!

And this is entirely due to the courage of Christians like Aida and to the vision of Michael Bourdeaux, an Anglican clergyman who had faith enough to follow God's leading and go to enormous lengths to 'see for himself' certain facts reported in a letter which reached him through roundabout ways from unknown, desperate, trusting hands. In time that letter would multiply into hundreds of letters from believers of all denominations all over Eastern Europe. The facts it set out simply and sincerely of harassment, persecution and destruction would be repeated over and over again and be relayed by telex to the world from a charming building, once a primary school, set among trees and fishponds, beside a wooden windmill in an English village, part of London's affluent green-belt area. Michael Bourdeaux himself is a Cornishman, and a music lover who umpires at Wimbledon! Michael has seen his work grow from a personal file to a research centre with a team of highly qualified workers, fluent in many languages with a network of dedicated support extending to Singapore and Australia as well as throughout Europe.

And the converted village school, which stores file after file recording situations so nightmarish that they seem almost like a horror film, is called Keston College. Here, amidst trees with their changing leaves, visited by squirrels, the occasional London Transport bus and visitors from all over the world, is a group of people from diverse backgrounds who make it their aim to 'tell the world', just as Aida begged. Gradually, perceptibly, the world is awakening and, compelled by fear at the terrible uncertainties which face us all, and disturbed by the spiritual vacuum which makes so much modern living an emptiness at the core, we in the West are beginning to listen. And the prayers of literally thousands of believers, Orthodox, Baptist, Lutheran, Pentecostal, Catholic, Jew are being answered.

They pray, not for themselves, desperate though their need is, but for us complacent Westerners who take for granted

to be a psychiatric examination, after which he
was unsuitable for military service for 'ideological
y April he had been registered as a psychiatric
hout his knowledge. (Doctors later told his wife,
hat Valeri 'is not really ill' but his views and
r from 'normal Soviet views' and so he stands 'in
atment'.[1]) This judgement deprived Valeri of his
river. Since May 1983 he has had long periods
gular paid employment, a severe pressure on his
ddition to other harassments. His daughters, aged
d twelve, were followed to school, their home was
watched and in June the elder girl Zhanna was
by an official who called while Valeri was out
nded to know why her father was not working.
was frightening and confusing enough, but even
the family was the attitude of their own congre-
leri's great following among the young, his obvious
an evangelist had won him some respect, but his
k music, his vision for the unity of all Christians
nconventional, uncompromising methods fright-
hurch leadership. Hiding behind a facade of rigid
n the leaders, under pressure of the KGB, refused
t Valeri. 'Young people shouldn't be infected by
n the West,' he was told, despite the fact that many
nverts in the congregation are there precisely be-
hat music. Just when Valeri and his family most
hristian fellowship, prayer and support, he was
rom the Baptist church. In July 1983 he wrote a
letter to Keston describing his feelings about the
f his own church leaders. His closing words were:
important thing is that we should pray that God
His purpose through us . . . Do not fear for us, we
hands of Jesus.'
time part of 'His purpose' had already been ful-
racts from the rock opera had been broadcast back
iet Union, with an instant, overwhelming response.
ng people, wanting to know more about the Christ-
which pulsed triumphantly through the music,
aleri. Letters came from all over the Soviet Union
himself commented, 'It is as if the cry of the spirit

our heritage of religious freedom with its wealth of Christian
literature.

This is a book about people both in the West and in the
countries of Eastern Europe who affirm a living God denied
by totalitarian governments and dethroned by the rule of
market forces in Western materialism. It is about people
who have salvaged from the rubble of a Christendom all but
destroyed by totalitarianism, on the one hand, and shallow
complacency on the other, a pearl of very great price: the
Christian hope which sustains us all. It is about people
whose faith triumphs in a society which denigrates believers
and indeed actively destroys them in its avowed commitment
to remould humanity; and about people in a blinkered society which caters for human greed but belittles and ignores
the things of the spirit. Finally, this book is about people
whose faith redeems times which are dark indeed, and about
people who have made it their business to make that faith
known.

[1] Michael Bourdeaux and Xenia Howard-Johnston, *Aida of Leningrad*, Gateway Outreach 1972; paperback edn, Mowbray 1976.
Aida's words recall another outstanding Christian, the Orthodox
believer Anatoli Levitin: '. . . .atheism is not free, just as religion is
not free . . . Therefore the struggle for religious freedom is also a
struggle for the freedom of atheism, for methods of compulsion
(direct and indirect) are compromising atheism, depriving it of all
ideological significance and all spiritual fascination. Therefore, long
live free religion and free atheism.' (30 May 1965)
[2] See n. 1 above.

2

'A dear and difficult happiness'

People are beginning to understand that a desolate soul cannot be satisfied with alcohol, drugs, or even wealth ... We want to know about God. We need God.

Valeri Barinov

Christians all over the world must not ignore one single case of detention of dissidents or believers in psychiatric hospitals.

Father Gleb Yakunin (16 October 1965)

15 October 1983. It didn't just rain that day. It rained in buckets. Gale force winds savaged the yellowing trees around Keston College and lashed water on the fishponds to a churning mass with waves eighteen inches high. Or was it just nine? Keston College staff welcomed shivering visitors warmly all the same.

But even the staff weren't prepared for quite the number of people who had to be squeezed into the village hall, marshalled around the College, fed and looked after. They came from far and near and spoke quite a few different languages: Russian and Polish, Czech and Latvian, Gaelic and Norwegian. Some people had got up before dawn, others had travelled overnight. One distinguished guest, the Dean of Trondheim, had flown from Norway. There was a telegram from a Keston Support Group in Singapore and news of active groups in Australia as well. But the thing which drew so many people to Keston that atrocious day was highlighted by a photograph of a rock musician from Leningrad, Valeri Barinov. And the terrible news was broken. The 40-year-old singer, a self-taught musician whose one desire was to fill the empty lives of young people both in the Soviet Union and the West with the joy and peace which he himself had come to find in Jesus, had been arrested four

days before and interned in a Leningrad psych: because, as the district military commissio speaks of his role in the working of divin̦ the power of Christ and actively prea And in the psychiatric hospital Vale injected with harmful drugs.

Valeri Barinov became a Chr converted out of a vacuum whic alcohol and a 'drop-out' lifestyle. for the young people whose lives had been and who form an unac Soviet society, caught in a spiral behaviour, but completely denied

Having found his way out of th Jesus, Valeri could easily have ign he sought imaginative, creative a presenting Christian realities to d and composed a rock opera called ' contained a powerful gospel messa the task of getting the Russian lyric Having achieved this, he learnt the that one day this message would people throughout the world. Ev gether a group of talented musician iety of denominations, and then s miracle took place. The group ma plete secrecy their whole musical. needed to find an audience. They ci and copies of 'The Trumpet Call' sian eventually reached Keston Cc

By this time Valeri and fellow-n had brought down the wrath of their heads. Their open letter to preme Soviet of the USSR reques formances of the rock opera was from being allowed to go ahead w was promptly subjected to intimida the KGB. At the end of January was being called up to do two mo would therefore have to have a

need of job as a without re family in a thirteen ar constantly questioned and dema

All this worse for gation. Va power as use of roc and his ened the puritanism to suppor music fro young co cause of needed C expelled f poignant attitude o 'The mos will fulfill are in the

By tha filled. Ext to the Sov Soviet you ian faith wrote to V and Valer of our people is expressed in these letters—we want to know about God, we need God ... We are sick of the atheistic brochures which lie about on the shelves of our bookshops—we want the Holy book, the Bible.'

Then at 10.40 p.m. on 13 October came a call to Lorna, Michael's wife. A friend of Valeri's, himself under threat of arrest, phoned the Bourdeaux home. 'Is Lorna there?' the operator asked, but no connection was made. An agonizing wait followed. A heavy day lay ahead, but neither Michael nor Lorna could think about getting some rest, wondering if the caller would risk further trouble and try again, or if indeed he had already been silenced. Then twenty minutes later a second call came with the news of Valeri's arrest ...

It was against this background that the Open Day went forward. Lorna, who is one of the Keston staff, had her share of the preparations to do—as well as a host of things to be done at home with Saturday fully booked. But all that had to be dropped. Instead a telex must be drafted, informing the media about Valeri. Telephone calls followed. Newspaper articles were written, typed and delivered, publicity and posters were prepared for the Open Day.

And Valeri's hopeless fate, his photograph in the front of the crowded village hall, gave Michael's words, spoken to the accompaniment of the wind lashing rain against the steamy windows, an added force. 'The persecution of Russian Baptists is running at a higher level than at any time in the last twenty-five years. The number of arrests and *rearrests* is at its worst since Stalin,' Michael stressed. 'The harassment of all branches of the Christian Church and of Jewish believers is too little reported by the Western media.'

Indeed, the week before the Open Day took place the trial of Dr Iosif Begun, a 51-year-old engineer charged with 'anti-Soviet agitation and propaganda', had been held in a small ante-room of Vladimir prison, north-east of Moscow, where Dr Begun had been held incommunicado since his arrest eleven months previously. Dr Begun, whose application to emigrate to Israel was turned down, is a leader of the campaign to legalize the teaching of Hebrew in the USSR. On 14 October 1983 Begun received the maximum sentence, seven years in prison followed by five years in internal exile, but the British news media at any rate paid no attention to the Begun trial, nor to the arrest of two Czech priests. 'We must pay better attention to the whole subject of human rights,' Michael warned. In this fragile state of affairs the nomination of Lech Walesa for the Nobel Prize appeared a beacon of hope. And although stressful world situations plainly affect the Soviet treatment of Christian believers, the amazing thing is that, increasingly, Western Christians are aware that our own lives are enriched by East European Christians of every denomination. There were nods and murmurs of agreement all around the village hall as Michael said, 'Despite all their sufferings the Russian Church is managing to define and refine a religious role of relevance both to Soviet society and to ourselves.'

In fact, amidst so much that is fearsome and alarming in our time, the very existence of any religious life at all in a state which has seen sixty years of intense atheistic attack and relentless propaganda is a miracle. And that its existence should be documented, analysed and recorded is another amazing story in which cassettes, photographs, phone calls, appeals, heart-rending letters, slanderous newspaper reports, typewritten *samizdat*, heart-warming prayers, poems, paintings all play a part. Perhaps one of the most astounding things in all the wealth of material in the Keston College archives is a bundle of cloth, fold after fold after fold after fold of it closely covered with painstakingly accurate handwriting, the entire transcript, word for exact word, of the trial of Aida Skripnikova in 1968, written by her fellow-believers in the court-room, all unknown to the judge, despite his boast, carefully recorded on the cloth, 'I can clearly note what is happening in the court-room . . . what can you note down in such conditions?'[2]

But a greater source of wonder still is the radiant, God-directed life of Christians in Eastern Europe who allow themselves to be stripped of academic awards, position, prestige, honour, livelihood, family, even health, even sanity, even life itself. Their story, unfolded by Keston College in its daily work, is a story of revival and renewal as well as faith and courage. If we want to find where renewal lies we must look

12

to Poland and the Life-Light movement there; to Lithuania and the harrowed young face of Nijole Sadunaite, lit with a joy few Western Christians have ever glimpsed; to the Orthodox churches in the Soviet Union and especially one where packed standing crowds gathered to hear a white-bearded priest, now cruelly silenced; to a shack with a badly functioning radiator and a table littered with books and glasses of tea half-drunk in the enthusiastic debating of young Orthodox believers, eagerly exploring philosophical ideas of their own Russian thinkers, ideas which had been shut away in inaccessible libraries for more than half a century, but, filtering out by various means, quickened and inspired minds unsatisfied with official atheism. Many of these young believers are now in prison, among them long-haired Alexander, or Sasha, Ogorodnikov, in his mid thirties, eyesight failing, teeth rotted away, and Vladimir Poresh, who declared at his trial, 'You have seen the witnesses. They are all my friends, believers and unbelievers . . . Christ's warriors who will conquer the world for him!'[3] Another, handsome young Sergei Yermolayev, was arrested when he was only nineteen, and already he has a liver condition. A brief message to a Western Christian in 1981 said in his own English:

> My situation now is worse and alarminger than ever. It seems to me that the chiefs are going to give me back to the camp. It would be a real murder: cruel and longer murder! I hope only on the God's love and favour! I miss my mother, my home, my church, my friends and my city very much . . . Please pray for me and write me oftener. I am always waiting for your letters . . .

We must look too to a lonely grandfather whose gentle 53-year-old wife Zoya Krakhmalnikova was arrested and taken away from her holiday home at 4 a.m., and to the American Embassy in Moscow where seven Pentecostal believers from Siberia, now finally in the West, immured themselves for five uncertain years, an embarrassment to Soviets and Americans alike. We must look to the sad and sorry country of Czechoslovakia with its rolling hillsides and historic capital, where religious and cultural life is almost in suspension, and we shall find Frantisek Lizna, a priest whose whole life is so permeated with heaven that even his guards, to his complete incomprehension, treat him kindly. We shall see him in handcuffs make the sign of the cross in blessing over reverent young people to the embarrassment of the police, and later see him kneel alone all night in prayer in a cell with twenty-three criminals, four beds and a bucket, although he must work next day cutting glass. And we must look to the West to *émigrés* old and young whose hearts are still in homelands barred to them for ever, where they will never now worship in their own native language with their own people, because their government abused them and defamed them and finally forced them to go.

Their story is told by Keston College in press reports, telex and news service, its journal *Religion in Communist Lands*, its paper *The Right to Believe* and an increasing number of books. Some of their photographs hung in the village hall that rainy Open Day. Like Valeri Barinov, they were the reason, the sole and sufficient reason for that gathering in the quiet English village. Their faith strikes deep chords across time and space, language, political systems and national boundaries. For it is in the things of the Spirit, however differently we manifest them, that we human beings find our true identity. And in a few moving words Michael Bourdeaux summarized this deep unity as he described a Jewish prisoner celebrating Hanukah, the Festival of Light, all alone in a prison cell with a stub-end of a candle and insufficient wick. The prisoner, Anatoli Shcharansky, who had already completed six years of a savage thirteen-year sentence, suffers from various health problems, including heart disease, which have been worsened by his long and well-publicized hunger strike in protest against the deprivation of visits and letters. In a letter which he sent to his mother on the day of the Festival of Purim, Anatoli writes:

Last Hanukah I lit candles all eight nights. It was a real Hanukah light produced by a tiny piece of paraffin wick. Every night I had to cut it even into smaller pieces. I was afraid it wouldn't last for eight nights. But when the eighth night came, all those eight tiny candles were burning, burning as bright as on the first night. These eight candles

14

are like the past eight years of our lives. They symbolize such a dear and difficult happiness and an extraordinary experience. For those eight years I am infinitely grateful to Him who 'set us in the land of the living; He keeps our feet from stumbling. For Thou hast put us to the proof and refined us like silver' [Psalms 66: 9,10].

This celebration in prison turned out to be as joyous an affirmation of the goodness of God as in the days of Judas Maccabeus and the original Hanukah Feast. Then, after persecution and the desecration of the Temple, one cruse of holy oil was found with which to light the seven-branched candlestick, yet it was found to be sufficient for eight days, and so, equally amazingly, was Shcharansky's tiny wick, a truly 'extraordinary experience' as he affirms, and a 'dear and difficult happiness' indeed in the midst of deprivation.

Those words, 'dear and difficult happiness', in many ways summarize this book; because the work of Keston College, fraught with difficulties though it is, reflects the happiness which radiates from court-room and prison yard.

'This hall was filled with a constant sense of joy,' affirmed Vladimir Poresh at his trial. He was sentenced to five years in a strict regime labour camp followed by three years in exile. 'After the trial, when I heard you singing "Christ is risen", I knew that this trial was a real triumph. It was not a defeat but a victory for all of us,' he declared.

And sometimes there is the happiness of success, short lived though it often is, and tinged always with the knowledge that no 'case' ever really closes. The 'Siberian Seven' families emigrate, but at that very time Galina Barats, a Pentecostal active in the campaign for emigration, was sentenced to six years' strict regime camp and three years' exile.

But let us return to Valeri Barinov. Following the Open Day BBC Radio 4 broadcast an interview with Michael and with Dr Philip Walters, Director of Research at Keston College. Valeri was mentioned. *The Daily Telegraph* took up the story, which was also reported in Sweden and Norway. Church papers, including *The Baptist Times*, *Church of England Newspaper*, *Church Times* and *The Tablet* all printed the story. On Tuesday 18 October a phone call to Leningrad brought hopeful news. 'They've transferred Valeri to another ward and they've stopped injecting him.' On Thursday 20 October, exactly a week after the news of Valeri's arrest, came relief and happiness. 'Valeri is free!' Valeri, his family and friends were convinced that this amazing release so soon was a direct result of prayer and publicity in the West. But the happiness could only be short lived. Valeri's friend, Sergei Timokhin, who, although under great pressure himself, wrote an impassioned appeal to the Presidium of the Supreme Soviet on Valeri's behalf, was officially informed that criminal proceedings had been instituted against him. Sergei is a member of Valeri's rock band called, like the musical, 'The Trumpet Call'. He is a tailor, and neighbours alleged that he made and sold clothes privately, a crime in the Soviet Union. A rock musician in a psychiatric hospital arouses interest in the West. Who, in our world of instant fashion, is going to bother about a tailor and some allegedly illegal clothing? We can't even understand the problem! Besides, old news is no news. . . Or will there be support for Sergei Timokhin, the Leningrad tailor who risked his own safety for his friend?

Happiness can only be short lived when *Keston News Service* records the tragic fate of other Christians in psychiatric hospitals.

In September 1980 a 48-year-old Baptist believer from Ukraine, Vladimir Khailo, was detained in a psychiatric hospital after years of harassment during which time both Vladimir and his wife Mariya and their fifteen children have suffered discrimination, slander and persecution. Their eldest son Anatoli was sentenced to eight years in intensified regime camps on trumped up charges of rape, being offered his freedom if he would denounce his parents, which he refused to do. His sister was repeatedly attacked on her way home from the evening shift at 12.30 a.m., until in the end she had to give up her job. Two younger boys were forcibly removed to boarding school and so badly treated that one of them, Misha, said to his father, 'If you had not told us about God and I did not know there is eternal life I would have committed suicide here.' Defamatory rumours were circulated about the family. Their name was publicly slandered,

16

even in schools. The younger children, still at school, were beaten up, and finally their father was interned indefinitely in psychiatric hospital where he is being destroyed by treatment with drugs. His wife in a letter to 'the whole church and all children of God' writes:

My husband is strictly guarded. He wears prison clothing, all black, and his hair has been cropped. He is taken for a walk for one hour each day . . . they put him in a room where there were twenty-seven people. . . They had to climb over each other to get to their beds. Immediately they started to give out tablets so that the prisoners slept day and night.[4]

Only Mariya herself and the children over the age of sixteen were allowed to visit their father. After a month he had become completely unrecognizable because his skin had darkened as a result of the tablets and injections. Two months later the situation was even worse. In one dose Vladimir was given thirty tablets of haloperidol as a result of which his body swelled and his heart began to fail. He lost consciousness. Then he received a variety of injections until he now has constant heart pains, his hands refuse to function and he cannot lift his right arm. Another drug, triftazin, made his body contract, his eyes twitch and his mouth twist from side to side.

Just as disturbing is news of an evangelical Christian, Anna Chertkova. Anna is fifty-seven and has been in a hospital for the criminally insane in Tashkent for ten years. She seems to have been singled out for particularly harsh treatment, being refused correspondence with anyone but her mother and sister, and then only once a week on open cards. Meetings with relatives are held under heavy guard and Anna is constantly threatened that even these will stop altogether if she voices a single complaint. An eye witness reported:

There are spy-holes in the doors through which the orderlies observe the patients. You have to knock to go to the toilet, but you have to watch out how you knock! If you knock too loudly they curse you, too quietly and they

17

don't hear. Don't knock too often, don't complain. If you talk too much you get an injection of sulphazin which sends your temperature up to 40°C and you are immobilized. Anna got sulphazin because she does not believe in communism but openly believes in God. ... She is not allowed to talk to the patients about God, they threaten to isolate her (not that there is anywhere that she can be more isolated) and say that she is an enemy of the people.[5]

Anna's health is good, say her friends, but her mind is being destroyed by neuroleptic drugs.

There is no charisma here, just stark, horrific facts. Who will help Vladimir Khailo and Anna Chertkova in their living hell? An outstanding Orthodox priest, Father Gleb Yakunin, now in labour camp with stomach ulcers after being force-fed hot liquids, wrote an appeal to delegates of the 5th Assembly of the World Council of Churches in Nairobi in 1975 in which he said, 'Christians all over the world must not ignore one single case of dissidents or believers in psychiatric hospitals.' Yet, as Michael wrote sadly in *Risen Indeed*, when Father Gleb was sentenced to ten years in prison and exile Western public opinion barely rallied to his defence, even when he smuggled a letter from prison camp begging Michael to support imprisoned believers and announcing that he himself was beginning a hunger-strike so that he might be allowed a Bible to comfort him in his prison cell. (He was given a Bible after eighty days on hunger strike.) At least a group of clergy and others have formed a support group and pray and hold vigils on behalf of Father Gleb, while the Archbishop of Canterbury spoke on his behalf at the World Council of Churches Assembly in Vancouver in 1983.

No wonder happiness in Keston can only be short lived when such brutal persecution continues. Keston College translates, records and transmits these and similar stories. But who will pray and care for Alexander Ogorodnikov, Vladimir Poresh, the Khailo family and all the many, many others? Keston College is the voice for Christians who can no longer speak. We, who have voices, must listen and cry loudly on their behalf: 'Enough!'

[1] *Baptist Times*, 20 October 1983.
[2] Michael Bourdeaux and Xenia Howard-Johnston, *Aida of Leningrad*. Gateway Outreach 1972; paperback edn, Mowbray 1976.
[3] *Religion in Communist Lands*, vol. 10, no. 3, winter 1982.
[4] *Christian Prisoners in the USSR 1983–4*. Keston College 1983.
[5] Ibid.

3

'The quiet call of God'

And our ailing souls heard at last the quiet call of God.
                                        Alexander Ogorodnikov

With those words 26-year-old Alexander Ogorodnikov summed up the lifespring of renewal which has welled up in the midst of official atheism.

Reawakening has blossomed all over Eastern Europe. Young people in Poland, nurtured on a confusing conflict of values between church and school and home, have made what had seemed impossible become a living reality before the eyes of the whole world, through faith and prayer, heedless of the grave risks they ran. In Czechoslovakia, in the aftermath of a bleak betrayal of their nation, while many young people, trying to carve out a better future for themselves, have turned their backs on their homeland in despair, others have found faith flower amidst red stars and dreary officialdom. In East Germany, deeply repentant of the terrible capitulation of a previous generation to totalitarianism and mass murder, but with the brave example of the confessing Church and men like Dietrich Bonhoeffer, Christians consciously try to make atonement and work out the implications of the gospel in their situation. In the Baltic country of Lithuania a hillside of crosses, barbarously destroyed, symbolizes the fiery faith of young people who went one midnight, having received Communion, to plant a new cross there, despite surveillance, praying, 'Christ, our King, may your kingdom come to our country!'[1]

Each year the miracle of spring touches our northern lands, and it is always a wonder, and a cause for great gratitude, but perhaps nowhere more than in Russia, snowbound from November until April. Quietly the snow melts and the thaw begins. Young leaves unfurl in parks and boulevards, softening the severity of Soviet architecture. Blossom turns grey trees to dancing brides and the sound of running water brings chuckles of laughter to river banks and beds of streams as frozen rivers flow. No wonder spiritual renewal is often compared with the coming of spring which floods the entire land!

The snow has melted and water has poured forth . . . over the Russian land [wrote one young Christian breathlessly] . . . But atheism—muddy water, floods, the ice is breaking, rubbish of all kinds is being carried away. Spring is coming, the torrent . . . The torrent of thoughts—I cannot hold it back in my head, it has spilled out here on paper . . . Perhaps you too have been carried away by this torrent?

Perhaps, realizing dimly that we have 'reached the point of having more and more things and less and less joy in life', as Dostoyevsky puts it, we too are being carried towards the quiet call of God, which is our real health, an ever deepening 'inward sense of our living bond with the other world, with the higher, heavenly world', as Dostoyevsky makes his saintly Father Zossima say.

And if, thanks to the deep faith of persecuted Christians, we find our faltering trust strengthened and our love renewed, this too is the result of 'the quiet call of God' which came in an amazing way to Michael Bourdeaux via a letter from two unknown women.

Michael has sketched out his story with characteristic modesty in his remarkable book, *Risen Indeed*. As long ago as 1959 the way had opened up for him to become one of the very first postgraduate students to spend a year studying at a Soviet university on an exchange visit. That year made Michael sense God's leading in his life, for even in the atmosphere of fear and distrust he sensed the power of Russian Christianity, the deep fervent faith of the Baptists and the exultant soaring worship of the Orthodox. For one Easter midnight, in the sudden flare of thousands of candles, Michael saw in suffering eyes the joy of the risen Lord and read in worshipping faces the reality of the resurrection.

21

'How can they be so sure?' I asked myself. The answer always came back: they have trodden the way of the cross to the hill of Calvary . . . They do not debate the resurrection: they have experienced its reality in their own lives. They have not preserved their faith in hostile surroundings; it has preserved them. Their joy is truly a glimpse through the curtain which divides us from heaven.

Having once glimpsed heaven, although doubts and insuperable difficulties sweep back to cloud the vision, a person is ready to heed God's call. Michael set himself towards ordination and, as a young curate in his first parish, wrote a book about Russian Christians. It passed from editor to editor, rejected twelve times, but Michael persevered, and that alone speaks volumes both for him and his vibrant, lovely first wife, Gillian. Her strength and warmth nurtured the developing personalities of their two growing children. She coped with instant hospitality even though her dining-room was turned into Michael's office. Later she conjured up furniture for the derelict school which was to become Keston College, transporting all manner of unwieldy items on the roof of her car before hurrying home to give a dinner party and rush out to sing with the Philharmonia chorus. She charmed office equipment out of the blue, wrote marvellous letters, and finally fought cancer, enduring pain with great courage and faith until her death in 1978. Even in death her thoughts were with the work she had shared with Michael. At her request there were no flowers, but £8,000 flowed in to restore and refurbish the suite of rooms in the College now dedicated to Gillian.

'They were an amazing team,' comments Mavis Perris, for many years Michael's secretary, who has been involved in the work since she sat at a typewriter in the Bourdeaux dining-room and has watched it expand into archives and files in Keston College. 'If someone had told me that Gillian would die I would have thought Keston would die, but Michael kept going with immense courage.'

And Keston College kept going too, as Michael and his growing staff held on, learning in the midst of sorrow the reality of the resurrection, experiencing the triumph of faith

22

so often affirmed by the Christians whose voice their daily work transmits to all who will hear.

'An inner light tells us that Christ's crucifixion is already resurrection,' declared Father Dmitri Dudko, an Orthodox priest whose discussion-style sermons drew thousands of amazed people to stand in his crowded church in Moscow to listen and ask questions in public which they had never dreamed possible. 'Such a situation already in and of itself makes us better, more creative. As free creatures we are called to co-creation with the Lord. And look! The crucifixion of Christ in Russia today, the persecutions and the mockeries, lead to the resurrection of men's faith.'[2]

The reality of that faith drew Michael back to the Soviet Union in 1964. Two things encouraged him. First, a hopeful reply from Faber and Faber, who said that if he reworked his book and brought it up to date (which would mean a trip to the Soviet Union to gather relevant information) they might be interested in publishing it, as there was certainly very little written on the subject of religious life in the Soviet Union. And secondly, there was a much travelled letter, translated from Russian, which had made a long journey from Ukraine to Moscow and thence to Michael. The letter appealed to the Western world (just as Aida had tried to do) to do something to help a persecuted Church, and particularly to prevent the closure of the Pochayev monastery, an important religious centre in Ukraine where monks were already being humiliated, beaten up and harassed.

The letter had been written by two unknown women and was signed only with their surnames, and now Michael realized that he must become actively involved. Accordingly he booked a cheap trip to the Soviet Union that April. Of course it was good to be back in a country where increasingly he was aware of the voice of God through the lives and spirituality and sufferings of its people, but as far as new information went the trip proved a disappointment. In fact at that time Aida Skripnikova, who had already been in prison for a year, was facing rearrest and repeated slander ('twenty-four and mature in Christian suffering', as Michael was later to write[3]); while another Baptist, Georgi Vins, was emerging as a fearless leader, and relentless persecution pursued Christians of all denominations. But in a short visit to the Soviet Union little of that was apparent and Michael returned home with no new material for his book and no further news of the unknown writers of the letter which had burned its way into his heart.

Then quite unexpectedly, hard on the heels of that disappointment, came a chance to return to the Soviet Union on a free trip as a group leader, and there the unexpected happened and Michael met the very same women who had written the letter.

Friends in Moscow told him how the persecution had been stepped up in the three months since his last visit. A church Michael remembered from his student days had been blown up two weeks previously. 'You'd better go and see for yourself,' his friends advised.

Michael caught a taxi at once, and to save arousing suspicion stopped some distance away from what had once been a beautiful Moscow church. As he came closer he could see the square ahead of him, empty of everything except a twelve-foot fence, completely blocking the view of what might lie behind it, but a slight hill up a side street afforded a glimpse of twisted metal on tumbled masonry. Then, in the fading daylight Michael noticed the dumpy figures of two elderly women. One was trying to hoist the other up to peer through a crack in the fence at the desolation concealed behind the high boards.

Michael longed to go and talk to the women. His friends had already told him how the authorities had herded believers out on to the street where they had promptly surrounded their beloved church in a protective ring. But in spite of the risk of life involved the soldiers had let off their dynamite charges. Perhaps the two elderly ladies had been in the congregation that day and had returned to the square to see for themselves the sorry ruin which had so recently been a place of worship?

He was too discreet to approach the women in the square, which was almost certainly still under surveillance. He waited until they had finished their sad inspection, followed them carefully as they walked away and then caught them up with a polite, 'Excuse me, please. Can you tell me what's been going on over there?'

They jumped back as though they had received an electric shock and looked at the curly-haired young-man in amazement. Trying to alleviate their fears, Michael said gently, 'Don't worry. If you're afraid to talk to me I'll go away at once.'

'Who are you?' they asked.

'A foreigner,' Michael said. 'I've come here because I'm interested in your church and I want to find out what's been happening.'

'A foreigner? You're the very person we need,' one of them declared, putting her hand on Michael's shoulder. 'Come with us. We must talk to you.'

So Michael followed the two women out to the suburbs. He didn't try to talk to them again. They walked to a bus stop, caught a trolley-bus and then a tram right to the edge of the city with never a word spoken. All three must have been praying hard, certain that God had brought about this strange meeting, although Michael had no idea who the women were or they who he was.

None of them was prepared for what happened next.

They reached their destination: an upstairs room in an old wooden house, soon to be swallowed up by modern housing. It was set among trees with the first hint of summer's end yellowing their leaves. A third elderly lady, the owner it turned out of the flat, was waiting for them. To Michael she seemed just like the other two, little and stout.

'See what God has brought us!' one of the women declared, introducing Michael to her friend. 'It's a young man from abroad.'

'I'm English,' Michael said, still trying to prevent any fear on the part of the elderly women. 'I've studied here and I met Christians then. But recently I've been hearing that the persecution of the Church has been getting worse and I decided to take a trip to Moscow to see if there was anything I could do to help my friends.'

'How wonderful . . . but what exactly brought you here?' persisted his hostess, almost as though she could hardly take in what she heard.

'Well . . . I've got a document,' Michael began.

'A document?'

'A letter,' Michael explained. 'It came to me from Paris, but it was really from Pochayev.'

The three women exchanged incredulous glances. 'Who wrote it?' one of them demanded.

Michael hesitated. How much should he tell? Could he really trust these unknown women? But he needed their help. He hoped they were going to be honest with him in their turn. Besides, it was obvious that they were deeply involved in the fate of the persecuted church. He took a deep breath: 'Two women . . .' he began.

'Who were they?'

'There were only two surnames on the letter,' Michael recalled. 'Nothing else, not even an initial.'

'What were the two names?'

'Wait a minute, let me think; oh yes, Varavva was one and the other one was Pronina.'

The awestruck silence which followed this announcement was broken by uncontrollable sobbing. Uneasily Michael wondered what was wrong. Perhaps he'd been unwise, after all, in mentioning those two names. Then, struggling with her tears his unknown hostess sobbed out an explanation: 'My two guests here . . . they're not from Moscow, you know . . . they're from Ukraine. They're the very people who wrote that letter.'

Now it was Michael's turn to stare in disbelief. Could it really be true . . . but, laughing and crying together, they were introducing one another.

'This is Feodosia Varavva. She wrote . . .'

'I'm the one who wrote the appeal. And here's Pronina, my friend. She signed it.'

'We travelled all the way to Moscow with it. We needed to find a foreigner . . .'

'We were looking for someone who would agree to take the letter with them when they went back home . . . Of course we couldn't send it, and anyway we don't know anyone outside our own country . . .'

'But we knew we'd be more likely to find someone here in Moscow. We searched around for days. . . '

'And eventually we met a French lady who spoke Russian. We asked her if she'd be so kind. . .'

'And she took our letter. Did you meet her?'

'No.' Michael added his own explanation. 'She sent the letter to a friend of mine in England who sent it on to me. I came back here as quickly as I could to find out more news, but my first visit was quite unsuccessful. Then the chance came quite unexpectedly for me to make a return trip.'

'God has sent you to us,' the old ladies declared. 'It's six months since we wrote that letter and things have got worse, much much worse. They're even putting monks into psychiatric hospitals. We've written more documents. Some of the monks have written some too. We've brought them to Moscow with us.'

'We only arrived this afternoon. We were going to try to find another foreigner, someone else who might take a letter, but our friend here told us about the terrible things that have been happening in Moscow itself.'

'I told them about the church and they went out to have a look and see what happened. They met you!'

Once again there was silence. The sky had darkened, while inside the simply furnished room four people, now no longer strangers, faced each other in the dusk. And it was then that Michael heard the quiet call of God.

'They met you.' They had travelled 700 miles, he had travelled more than 2,000, and there, in the heart of Moscow, against all the odds, they'd met. Of course it was God's doing! Only the Holy Spirit could have brought about the amazing coincidence. And Michael knew that he would have to help his friends. How could he not? Of course he would take their letters. But having taken them, what then? Who would listen to an unknown young clergyman? There were no organizations that he knew of who would serve the persecuted church. Well, then, he would have to do it himself. He was thirty, young enough to do and dare, mature enough not to be too rash. But what about his family? Who would pay the bills? What would Gillian say when he told her that his work from now on was to let the voice of the silenced church be heard? Yet how could he possibly turn his back on the needs of Christians in prison, in psychiatric hospitals? His own parishioners had a building to worship in and they would soon find another curate to serve them. What about the Moscow congregation who had so valiantly tried to prevent the destruction of their beautiful church? Who would speak for them? Who?

'I could never contemplate ignoring such a call,' writes Michael simply.[4] And so the quiet old-fashioned flat in a wooden house in a Moscow suburb saw the first beginnings of what was to become Keston College as the Englishman said a silent 'yes' to three Russian voices and to the secret workings of the Spirit which know no boundaries of time and place so long as faith exists, even a modicum, even the size of a mustard seed.

It is, after all, says Jesus, the tiniest seed of all which grows into a tree large enough to provide nesting places for the birds to rear their young. In Keston village itself new shoots spring from an ancient oak, the 'Wilberforce Oak' it is called, because nearly 200 years ago William Wilberforce, the reformer, visited Keston. The oak still stands as a symbol of freedom where once Wilberforce discussed the problems of black slaves in white colonies with the Prime Minister, William Pitt, who lived in the village, and persuaded him to stand out against the powerful property owners of the day in the interests of human liberty. And today Keston College supports the right to believe, a basic right which is still only too obviously denied. A leading and celebrated Russian dissident, Dr Andrei Sakharov, estimates that there are 10,000 prisoners of conscience in the Soviet Union, of whom about 2,000 are religious believers, including Jews and Muslims, as well as Jehovah's Witnesses. 307 prisoners are currently known to Keston College, but it is certain that there are very many more prisoners of every denomination, perhaps up to 1,500, whose cases are not known.[5] Add to this the increasing number of believers who are detained indefinitely in psychiatric hospitals, certified as insane, and the reason for Keston's continuing work is obvious.

Christians in prison, too, seem to be singled out for particularly harsh treatment. For instance, *Keston News Service* (17 November 1983) reports that Eduard Bulakh, a Pentecostal Christian from Lithuania, was locked up in the labour camp punishment cell because his hair was said to be too long. This is particularly ludicrous as prisoners have their hair shaved regularly and Eduard had been in prison for over two years, although his original sentence was for one year. However, when Eduard had completed his first sentence in 1982 he wasn't released. Instead he was placed under investigation, retried and sentenced to a further two and a half years in a strict regime camp. Earlier in 1983 the 42-year-old father of three had suffered a heart attack and, more recently, collapsed after being beaten up and left lying unconscious and unattended.

Fearing greatly for her husband's health, his wife Svetlana travelled to the labour camp. She arrived at the camp on 27 October but was turned away without being allowed to see her husband.

'Your visit's cancelled,' she was told. 'He's in the punishment cell.'

Horrified, Svetlana learnt that her husband had been in the punishment cell for almost a month and still had a week to endure. Her journey had been in vain and her husband and she had been denied a few precious moments together— and for such a trivial, ridiculous reason! The whole story seems too absurd to be true, but its very absurdity highlights the tragic suffering of one believing family who can see no future for themselves under a regime which denies them the right to believe.

Perhaps the one glimmer of hope which exists for the Bulakh family and the other 306 prisoners on Keston's list is that three weeks after Svetlana was turned away from the labour camp this fact was reported in *Keston News Service*. The network of information holds good, something Aida longed to see. And this is because Michael Bourdeaux sacrificed his own financial security and, armed with letters from two elderly Ukrainian women and some Orthodox monks from a vandalized monastery, set off for London once more with a new purpose in his mind: to alert the Western world about the true picture of religious life in Communist countries. Michael took his work to various centres of Russian studies and quickly found stalwart supporters in Sir

John Lawrence, now the President of Keston College, and an eminent specialist in Soviet politics, Professor Leonard Schapiro of the London School of Economics, whose death in the autumn of 1983 robbed the College of a dear and distinguished friend.

Soon small groups of interested people began to look to Michael's work for the amazing evidence of faith and trial in the least likely place of all: the Soviet Union, where, it was still commonly felt, Lenin, not God, reigned. No wonder Michael called his next major book *Faith on Trial in Russia*. Published in 1971, it is a highly readable, challenging study of the early beginnings of the Christian human rights movement, centred around the Baptist leader, Georgi Vins. *Faith on Trial* makes an enormous impact on its readers. Particularly moving is the unforgettable story of a family whose mother Nadezhda Sloboda had become a Christian through listening to radio broadcasts. She and her husband were both farm workers. Two of their daughters, Galina aged eleven and Shura aged nine, were removed to a state boarding institution because they were being brought up as Christians. On 11 February 1966 Nadezhda and her husband were sentenced to the loss of their parental rights, condemned by the state as being unfit to bring up their children who, however, were put away into appalling conditions. In the institution they both developed head lice and scabies. Their heads were shaved. Galina's feet were infected and suppurating because she was forced to wear unsuitable, damp footwear. Worse still the children were not allowed to receive letters from their parents. In the end, nearly two years after being removed from home, the two sisters ran away.

Aida knew Nadezhda Sloboda and refers to the girls in her own trial.

They ran home in such heavy frost that their mother was frightened. 'Weren't you really frozen?' she asked. But the children replied, 'We kept on running and running, we stopped, and rubbed our knees and ran on again.' The mother asked the younger girl, 'Didn't you cry a bit from the cold?'

'What are you thinking about, Mummy,' said the little

girl, amazed. 'How could we cry at such a happy time? After all, we were running home!' The children lived at home for a month and didn't want to go to bed without their mother, so all the time they slept in the same bed as their mother.[6]

But the children's happiness lasted only a month. In an incident reminiscent of a crude Punch and Judy show they were kidnapped from their classroom during school hours.

The village policeman had been hiding behind a cupboard. He pounced on Galya [= Galina (diminutive)] and dragged her out to a police car. Screaming for help Galya put up a valiant fight, so much so that the policeman fell in the struggle, but kept hold of his terrified prisoner. Shura was kidnapped too and the car drove away to the accompaniment of the terrified screams from the two helpless girls.[7]

And when they next returned home, almost a year later, there was no mother for them to snuggle beside in bed. Nadezhda Sloboda was sentenced on 11 December 1968 to a prison term of four years. The heartbroken girls themselves added a letter to other similar pleading documents sent to Brezhnev himself and to the West by a newly-formed 'Union of Christian Baptist Mothers', whose development Michael traced in print for the first time in the West in *Faith on Trial*.

But even in prison Nadezhda's faith sustained her. Kept for one month in freezing conditions in an unheated cell, clad only in a summer dress and fed with bread and tepid liquids, Nadezhda rejoiced, 'The Lord kept me warm', finding as her daughters had done, that when the road leads Home and the mind is filled with loving thoughts even freezing cold ceases to be a torment and suffering is eased.

The publication of *Faith on Trial* coincided with Michael's efforts to set up a Centre for the Study of Religion and Communism which was soon to produce a journal edited by Xenia Howard-Johnston, the first of Michael's helpers on the research team. The journal furthered Michael's work, but apart from his own research fellowship and a widening circle of support there was very little income. No British

Christian Church of any denomination saw fit to give a grant towards work on behalf of persecuted Christians of every denomination, although some individual congregations did give generously. Michael worked tirelessly and his staff grew from Kathy Matchett and Mavis Perris, who is still cheerfully involved in the work of Keston College on the secretarial side, to a team proficient in almost a score of languages. But impressive though this is, it is still not nearly enough to cover the enormous area of the work as China opens up.

There are, however, two languages which are truly international: the language of pain and the language of hope. 'We're never alone or rejected, not even in prison,' declares Aida. Her words are repeated by countless Christians until, in the end, we begin to listen too and catch the echoes of a living faith which may yet save our sad world from destruction.

[1] Michael Bourdeaux, *Land of Crosses*. Augustine Publishing Co. 1979.

[2] Dmitri Dudko, *Our Hope*. St Vladimir's Seminary Press 1977. This collection of sermons alone has inspired and encouraged countless Christians in Eastern Europe and in the West.

[3] Michael Boudeaux, *Faith on Trial in Russia*. Hodder and Stoughton 1971.

[4] Michael Bourdeaux, *Risen Indeed*. Darton, Longman and Todd 1983.

[5] *Christian Prisoners in the USSR 1983–4* (Keston College 1983) and *Aid to Russian Christians Newsletter*, no. 35, winter 1983.

[6] Michael Bourdeaux and Xenia Howard-Johnston, *Aida of Leningrad*. Gateway Outreach 1972; paperback edn, Mowbray 1976.

[7] Bourdeaux, *Faith on Trial*. See n. 3 above.

'Joy which puts lions off-balance'

There can be no joy without our willingness to complete in
ourselves what the Church has yet to suffer, so that the Bride
may be pure and ready . . . I assure you that our suffering
and joy are so carefully balanced that I can perceive in them
the guiding hand of our good and merciful Lord.

Father Frantisek Lizna

Over the years the research work which Keston College has
been able to undertake has varied according to the interests,
expertise and specialities of the people who have joined Michael in his work. In the last few years a store of useful
information about Czechoslovakia and Poland has been collected thanks to the efforts of two of the research staff, Alexander Tomsky and Grazyna Sikorska.

Alexander himself is Czech. His Jewish father survived the
war. His Polish mother, caught up in the mêlée of homeless
fleeing people in post-war Europe, found herself trapped in
Czechoslovakia, unable to travel to her own homeland, in
spite of all her efforts. Cut off from Poland for ever, she
passed its language to her son and Alexander is fluent in
both Czech and Polish. Russian, of course, is obligatory in
the schools of Eastern Europe, while at home his father, at
odds with the post-1948 regime, habitually listened to radio
programmes from Austria rather than the state-controlled
Czech radio, so that Alexander grew up with some understanding of German.

His desire was to be a journalist, and his work at Keston
has enabled him to use his journalistic interests to the full.
He writes knowledgeably and vividly in a compelling fluent
English, with control and excellence a native speaker might
envy.

Pre-Dubcek Czechoslovakia enjoyed a level of material well-being neighbouring Poland lacked, but a drab uniformity of thought and a strict censorship of the press stifled independent life. Polish films of the early sixties were creative, poetic and often very beautiful, though too many perhaps inevitably were about the war. Nazi atrocities were frequently allowed to point political rather than humanitarian morals; but, all the same, the best films shone with a luminous spirituality, while, by contrast, Czech films were mostly boring caricatures, naively critical of the West. Polish students of the period jived and danced the 'twist' in crowded cafes, raved about the Beatles and what they called 'big beat' music. Czech young people heard only the tired strains of unoriginal jazz and travelled to work in trains and trams decorated with the red star. The Polish intelligentsia could read all the major Western newspapers in special press clubs; the only paper from the British press easily available in Czechoslovakia was the Communist party paper, *The Daily Worker* (now *The Morning Star*).

A Polish joke of the time, one of hundreds which got bandied around, neatly sums up the situation. A Polish dog met a Czech dog at the border. 'Where are you going?' asked the Czech dog. 'Me? Oh, I'm off to Czechoslovakia to get some sausage,' the Polish dog replied. 'What about you? Why on earth are you going to Poland?' 'So that I can bark my head off in freedom,' answered the Czech dog.

In an unsmiling, heavily censored world Alexander, searching for deeper realities, found the freedom of discussion he and his contemporaries craved in a Jewish youth group. It was stimulating at first, but he needed another kind of spirituality which would involve more than the solidarity and comradeship of a small ethnic group. Besides, although they talked more freely over a wider range of topics than any other group he had met, they couldn't give him the answers he longed for. Nor could his own parents help. The stultifying atmosphere of the fifties which disabled the Czech Church, both Protestant and Catholic, and threw the ablest priests and pastors into prison, left a legacy of fear, and drove perhaps seventy-five per cent of the population into at best a nominal type of religious belief, a vague nod God-wards at festival times, perhaps, if even that. And yet the impoverished straits to which all cultural and intellectual life had been reduced left their own dissatisfactions, not least a sense that there must be more in life than the purely so-called scientific materialistic view of the world propounded as the only norm by official Communism. Crippled though the Church had become, weakened, restricted and almost totally controlled by the state, it nevertheless offered authentic values, extending even beyond the purely religious, so that it has become for many young Czechs a symbol of hope and resistance, gaining in credibility the more it has suffered.

But Alexander had no time to think his position through. While he, along with many like-minded intellectuals, still groped a questioning way towards a glimmer of faith, the dramatic events of 1968 overtook them all. Alexander returned home one evening to find his mother at the door and his bag packed. 'The Russian tanks are here. Go at once. It's all arranged,' she said, her quick action taken in the light of her own experience of the Soviet invasion of her native Poland in 1939.

So Alexander went. A visiting diplomat who frequently commuted between Prague and Vienna drove him and two total strangers right through the customs at the border with a wave to the guards, who knew him well, and on into the West, where Alexander washed dishes, worked in pubs and factories, gained two degrees and found the faith he had been searching for, becoming a Catholic. He married a Jewish girl he had met in the youth group. She had come to England as part of her studies and she too had become a Catholic in her own quest for reality. Now Alexander, fearing for the moribund culture and ruined Church in his homeland, works for the renewal of both. His articles and booklets on religious and cultural life in Poland and Czechoslovakia both inform and challenge, while his short profile of the saintly priest Father Frantisek Lizna is profoundly moving.

And now perhaps it is time to take up Father Lizna's story in a country where suffering has minimized the denominational barriers which are such a scandal in church life in the West. Christians in Czechoslovakia, both Catholic and Protestant, know what it is to make a stand for their faith even at the cost of their freedom, their status and their professional life.

Yet even so, it often seems for many Czechs that the only hope for a better, truer future for themselves and their families is to flee to the West, beginning life in a foreign country with nothing except the clothes they stand up in and a conviction that freedom matters more than their homeland itself, much though they love it. (One young Czech lad, uneducated and with no knowledge of Christianity except that his family always fasted until evening on Christmas Eve and then ate the carp they had stored for days in the bath, came to a Western city with literally nothing. With his first payment of breadline money he bought two T-shirts and two cassettes of music, one by Dvorak and 'Ma Vlast', 'My Homeland', by Smetana.)

But although Father Lizna was offered the chance to emigrate he chose to stay in his own country and be put into prison. 'Why should I emigrate?' he is reported to have said, 'Our prisons are greatly in need of a priest!'

But Frantisek Lizna's acquaintance with Czech prisons occurred in his early teens, years before he had any thought of becoming a priest, when he tore down a Soviet flag in a brave gesture of lonely protest. For that 'crime' he had to spend eight months in prison, with the result that, when he did his compulsory military service, he had to serve two years in a special punishment corps. This was so demoralizing that Frantisek tried to flee the country which had treated him so harshly, but he was caught and condemned in 1964, this time to two years in prison. But this new punishment brought about a spiritual awakening for the young prisoner. In the labour camp he met Christians, some of them church leaders, bishops and members of religious communities, banned in 1950. None of them had any hope of release, having been incarcerated in the terror of the fifties, and many of them, particularly those who had been superiors in their orders or communities, were not in fact released until the brief liberalization of 1968.

While he was still in prison Frantisek Lizna realized that God's hand had been in all his misfortunes. There would be no running away now. He would remain among his own people and serve them as a priest.

But ten testing years lay ahead before his calling would be realized. He had to study, and seized the chance to travel in 1968. He spent some time in Austria and in England in houses belonging to the Jesuit Order of which he is now a member, but, having heard that it was now possible for him to study for the priesthood in Czechoslovakia itself, he returned home in 1969, even though it was to a country occupied by the Soviet army. He trained at a seminary which was under constant pressure from the authorities to compel its ordinands to toe the line, either with promises of an easy parish or simply by intimidating them outright into joining the government controlled organization for priests.

Against a background of harassment as new austerities bit harder, the regime launched a series of bitter attacks in the press against the Church. It is a marvel that Frantisek Lizna survived his training uncorrupted, and a greater miracle still that he was allowed to be ordained at all, but, amazingly, he was consecrated as a priest in 1974. However, the authorities plainly realized their mistake. On the very day of his first Mass his licence to work as a priest was refused him. Without this licence he could not be given a parish to work in and could never now legally celebrate Mass.

It must have been a terrible blow to Father Lizna, but he could see that God was in control, in spite of everything. For he had been ordained by the Church as a priest and if the government forced him into manual employment, he would be a priest there, among workers and young people who might well never meet a Christian otherwise.

And indeed at work Father Lizna's life spoke so clearly that many people turned to him with problems and spiritual needs. He had an amazing ministry among the young, particularly those who were alienated by the schizophrenic life the state imposed upon them. The slim, dark-haired priest saw his calling to be identified particularly with the dregs of society, the drop-outs and those rejected by the establishment.

'He did his best to affirm his priesthood in everything he

37

did and said,' writes Alexander in the profile published by Keston College. 'His slightest gestures began to be controlled so that no one in the hospital where he was forced to work could have mistaken him for anything but a priest.'

Soon the Security police began to spread malicious slander about him, saying that he was an agitator who had caused wilful damage at work and, turning against him the very priesthood the state denied him, alleged that he had broken his vows of celibacy. The police followed him closely, often into unheated churches where they shuffled on hard pews while the man they spied on knelt and prayed.

Forced to work from fifty to sixty to seventy hours a week at heavy, poorly paid work no one else wanted to do, Father Lizna frequently did other people's work as well as his own. Once, under the influence of drink, a colleague confided in Frantisek that he had been planted there as an informer to keep an eye on the gentle, unassuming priest. 'I'll prove it's true too,' he boasted and, to show how well trained in karate he was, he started to break up the hospital furniture. The whole thing seemed likely to get out of control, when Frantisek quietly took over his drunk colleague's work load, rejecting all suggestions that the man should be reported.

Frantisek was never in the forefront of the human rights movement though he added his signature to Charter 77, an important human rights manifesto, and wrote a few outspoken letters to the authorities, pleading for the abolition of the death penalty, for prisoners to be allowed to have Bibles in their cells, and for himself to be allowed to work as a priest. He felt he had a duty to protest because, as he himself had doubtless learnt from Christians in the camps, 'The terror of the fifties was possible only because so many of us did not protest.' For the same reason he became involved in the clandestine production of sorely needed Christian literature. He was arrested, taken away in handcuffs, charged with illicit trading.

Repeated spells in prison have only increased Father Lizna's credibility and although he has never been allowed to carry out pastoral duties officially his personal piety and dedication have made him a symbol of spiritual integrity.

He is a Christian, burning with love for God [wrote some of his friends]. Do you know how he celebrated the anniversary of his religious vows? He returned to the shrine where he had taken his vows and there spent the night in meditation, in the open air, under the statue of Calvary: he then went straight back to work in the morning. His generosity knows no limits. Whenever anyone has asked him for anything, he has always tried to help, even at the expense of his own studies or sleep. Despite this, he always finds time for prayer. He prays at least two hours a day, often instead of sleeping.

At his trial crowds of young people gathered outside the court-room. They were not allowed inside, but, even so, the whole thing was an affair of intense embarrassment, not to Father Lizna himself, who radiated dignity, gentleness and calm, but to the unnerved authorities who rushed the trial through. After all, as one of his former lawyers pointed out: 'It is Father Lizna's insistence on his priestly vocation which seems at the root of the authorities' quarrel with him, rather than the dissident activity of which they accuse him.' For unlike other dissidents he never insisted on his own rights, or bothered to point out any glaring legal discrepancies, but his mere presence in the court-room exposed the whole thing as a farce, and made the cynical uneasy, while the young people who waited outside were drawn to him because of their own spiritual hungers and yearnings. As he was led away he lifted his manacled hands to bless his young friends, to the acute discomfort of his guards, turning a situation which had been planned to humiliate and silence him into a moment of great spiritual joy and triumph. The young people caught the meaning immediately and burst into song. 'Christ the victor has risen, rejoice!' they sang joyfully, annoying the authorities still more intensely.

Father Lizna's name became well known in the West, particularly in Austria, and a subsequent trial when he was charged with 'damaging state interests abroad' resulted in a wave of protests. At least 10,000 people, including members of Amnesty International, as well as fellow-Jesuits and scores of other Western Christians, pleaded on his behalf to the state authorities. Their appeals were rejected, but Father Lizna's sentence was unusually light: seven months in a labour camp. In spite of cramped, unsavoury living conditions and exhausting working hours, Father Lizna wrote letters, which at first seemed so unimportant to the prison authorities that they let them pass. But the letters express such joy and trust that they soon began to circulate all over the country. Like their writer, the simple unassuming words seem quite unremarkable, yet throb with an intense, compelling power.

> Our joy in the Resurrection is so central to our faith that it can be expressed any time and in any situation. The joy is with us even in the face of the lions' jaws ... Is it not marvellous, yet mysterious, to find that Christians radiate a joy which puts even the lions off-balance?

Alas, all too soon 'the lions' regained their balance. Predictably reacting with denial and punishment, the authorities forbade Father Lizna to write any more letters or to receive parcels or visitors. Pressure from the West lifted this prohibition, but Father Lizna's outgoing mail was so heavily censored he was forced to abandon all attempts at letter writing. His mother, on holiday in England with his sister, who now lives here permanently, sent a parcel which her son was not allowed to receive. Instead the badly messed-up contents were returned to England with a note to say that they were not properly wrapped. In addition Mrs Lizna was forced to pay £7 postage as the parcel had been returned without any stamps.

Early in 1983 the German Red Cross investigated the Plzen-Bory camp where Father Lizna was held and declared prison conditions to be appalling, 'worse than in the 1950s', both in the overcrowded insanitary cell shared by twenty-four men, and in the insufficiently ventilated workroom where glass dust from the cutting machines was an unacceptable health hazard.

Yet of these conditions Father Lizna writes (25 April 1982):

It is the third Sunday after Easter, a beautiful morning. Soon the sun will penetrate our cell, so that we can see again for ourselves that the good God never forgets us . . . As I hear the rattle of mugs from the corridor I realize that not only my eyes, but my ears too were created to testify to the truth of him who reigns above all, yesterday, today and forever. I am even now amazed how quietly the sun comes to us, without arousing the slightest attention, in great contrast to human behaviour. . . I would like to extend my brotherly greetings to the newly discovered particles of dust, hated here by everyone . . . See how the dust glitters! . . . Our eyes suddenly see the rays of the invisible world . . . From now on, that dust which until now has only been a reason for irritation and anger will have a spiritual significance for me. It will not only remind me of this cell . . . it will also invoke in me wonder at creation.

And of the cell itself he wrote in a previous letter (28 March 1982):

God, how frightening it is to see what prison reveals! How men, when forced into a corner, drop their last pretences and are prepared to don the most repugnant masks. My soul agonizes as I experience the truth that revelation brings with it the pain of suffering . . . This cell and these walls are so helpless. I am sure that St Francis would manage to talk to the cell as if it were a living thing. He would be sorry for it enduring so much foul language from its inhabitants as they kick it mercilessly. I am glad I almost managed to praise this cell when I was moved in here from conditions which were much worse. In all honesty it is quite large, remarkably warm and full of light. Really it is on our side. It lets in some spring air, it is like being in a desert but surrounded by God's bounty. It is by no means as gloomy and official as you imagine and if I say all these nice things about it, give thanks not to me but to God who looks after us so well.

At length the day scheduled for Father Lizna's release came, 28 June 1983. His mother and close friends travelled to the

41

prison camp to meet him, but the authorities came to his cell at dawn and took him secretly to Prague in a police van. There they deposited him, penniless but with an entourage of twelve policemen in civilian dress on his tail. Rather than compromise any of his friends, Frantisek slipped into a church where his friends actually found him when they arrived back in the city that evening. The policemen were there too, lined up in a pew behind him, while he unconcerned was making good use of an empty day, praying.

He left with his friends to a hopeless future, humanly speaking. For he was now unemployed, with no chance of even his orderly's job, while his hope of being officially licensed as a priest is now absolutely impossible. He has a 'criminal record' and is deemed totally unsuitable, but for Christians everywhere Father Lizna is an example of what it means to bear witness to the risen Christ, to rejoice in the midst of persecution and give thanks to God for everything.

Of himself Frantisek Lizna writes, 'It is my life's duty to work as a priest in the exclusive service of the Church and the gospel.' Perhaps it is significant that it is precisely the crushed, dispirited Czech Church which Father Lizna is called to serve, a Church which, however, shows us in the West, whose Christianity is too often little more than club membership, that true faith, as one Czech theologian puts it, 'fills the world with faith, hope and charity'.[1]

From this chapter it will be obvious that, weak and apologetic though our own faith often is, pressure from the West actively helps the persecuted church, reducing the severity with which the authorities deal with a particular person. Moreover, precisely as for Aida and the two indomitable elderly ladies from Ukraine who entrusted their precious letters to Michael, we are the only hope for our persecuted fellow-believers who otherwise experience only injustice. Terror, as Father Lizna himself pointed out, exists only as long as no one protests.

The persecuted church itself has increasingly found a new unity between the various denominations, and has drawn enormous encouragement from two things: the unprecedented developments in neighbouring Poland and the presence in the Vatican of a Slav Pope, a man who is thoroughly aware of Eastern Europe's difficulties and tensions, bred as he is in the faith which puts lions of all kinds off-balance. It is to Poland that we must now turn, and to Grazyna Sikorska whose life and witness in exile reflect her own deep faith and her loyalty to her countryman in the Vatican, Pope John Paul II himself.

[1] Father Josef Zverina, quoted in *Religion in Communist Lands*, vol. 8, no. 3, winter 1980.

5

'The freedom of God's children'

Through the disappointments and painful experiences which
past generations have endured and which the present generation unfortunately continues to experience, God is visiting
His people in a special way. This is also a sign, a sign of our
times, which we must interpret with great sensitivity and
readiness of heart.

Pope John Paul II (15 August 1980)[1]

Maybe the communist society is the highest goal towards
which the history of the world inclines, but for it not to
become the most terrible irony, the most lunatic despotism,
it must come about in a time when the light of Christ turns
everyone into a saint.

Zygmunt Krasinski (1846)[2]

Disasters, death, deprivation, turbulence and violence of all
kinds, whether natural or engineered by human inadequacy,
greed or vice shatter adults, but prove utterly devastating to
children whose faces age overnight as their eyes turn inwards
towards despair. We have already seen that policies overtly
committed to stamping out religious life turn ruthlessly
against children. A later chapter will unravel a web of violence and hypocrisy with a baby's corpse at the heart of it.
'. . . but it's better,' declared the authorities openly, 'that a
baby should die than be brought up by believers.'
   'The chief tragedy of atheistic society is the absence of any
human feeling, sympathy or compassion for people,' writes
Father Vasili Romanyuk, an Orthodox priest. Tragically, a
society avowedly committed to child care, providing clubs
and camps and culture in the form of children's theatre,
puppets, concerts and so on, as well as an annual 'International Children's Day', derides and vilifies children of be-

lievers, so that one adult Pentecostal Christian writes in despair:

> This is the introductory phase (for children) of our Christianity in USSR. There are the tears of frightened children. There is the feeling of disgrace when you are put to shame before children just like yourself, initiated to cry out in one voice 'Baptist, Baptist'. One must see with one's own eyes in order to understand those feelings which our children experience and which we experienced in our time.[3]

Children of believing parents are given low marks at school, denied entry into higher education, forced into poorly paid low-grade employment, and if they or their parents become involved in church life they bear the brunt of their Christian discipleship, being questioned at school, ridiculed and threatened.

'You degrade the honour of the Soviet school. We'll write a bad letter of reference,' one teacher scolded a schoolgirl in Lithuania who had read a religious poem at a fellow-pupil's funeral; and, true to her word, noted in the student's report 'she has not developed a materialistic outlook.'[4] Another girl, similarly, was noted as being 'deeply religious' and was refused entrance to higher education, even though she had the required grades, while even more sinister cases occur where some children are actually pressured by the authorities to become part of the security network.

And yet all over Eastern Europe church leaders witness the astonishing phenomenon of faith springing up in the lives of children and young people, so that Father Dmitri Dudko, an Orthodox priest, committed as he boldly declared 'to wage war on lukewarmness', notes with characteristic wonder, 'In Russia a resurrection from the dead is under way. Young people, who are always sensitive to contemporary processes of any sort, are interested in religion, and this can't be halted any more.'

In his sermons, which drew eager, if incredulous crowds, Father Dmitri movingly refers to the attempts by children to pray and express their love for Jesus, often thwarted by terrified parents. 'I've got a good job. I can't allow you to believe such nonsense!' mothers rage, aghast.

One story, told in Father Dmitri's inimitable manner, is worth repeating because it shows the pressure not only children, but the clergy too are under.

> Once an 11-year-old girl came to me for confession . . . I asked, 'Are you a sinner, child?' 'I'm a sinner,' she said with such a deep sigh! I think, 'What kind of sin can it be?' (The main thing is – what a sigh!) 'Well, so how are you a sinner, child?' 'It's like this,' she says. 'I believe, but they make me wear a Pioneer's tie. Isn't that a sin?' she asks me very fearfully. I even lifted up my head. If it had been a grown-up in front of me I'd have thought it was some kind of provocation, but since she was just a child it couldn't be. At any rate, I kept silent. The girl continues: 'Of course, we're powerless. They *make* us do it. So this is what we did. First we blessed it with holy water, and then put it on . . .' 'O, Lord,' I thought. 'How the Lord makes the children wise!' . . .
>
> It's both comical and painful. The question of faith is painful in school . . .[5]

Very telling in this extract is Father Dmitri's matter-of-fact explanation, 'I'd have thought it was some kind of provocation.'

Father Dmitri, as Michael Bourdeaux records in *Risen Indeed*, was moved from parish to parish, had both legs broken in a car accident, which was probably an attempt on his life, was arrested and forced to make a public confession and is now virtually silenced, although nominally free.

In his sermon Father Dmitri goes on to highlight the dilemma facing believers and their children. As he says 'the question of faith is painful in school.' In the West Christian young people may well utter a rueful 'Amen', but in totalitarian systems children find themselves forced into a dual existence, as Father Dmitri's little story illustrates, taught one thing at school and in the atheistic youth organizations and another at home. Children inevitably, warns Father Dmitri, 'grow up with a dual consciousness, and while continuing to believe do things which are utterly incompatible with faith.'

Perhaps Western parents, caught between Christian principles and the rampant materialism of our consumer society, may find a challenge in Father Dmitri's words, and with other Christian believers in Eastern Europe find relevance in the Polish people's fight to free themselves from self-deception. The Pope's parting message for the people of Poland, whose fraught situation he understood so well, was simply this: that they should speak the truth and live by the truth; words which are far from trite in an almost monolithic Catholic society, deeply characterized by dual standards since it fell under a communist regime at the end of the Second World War. Virtually all Polish children are baptized, yet until the Solidarity period the Polish Communist Party claimed some three million members. Even though the majority of them paid only lip service to the Party they still had to attend meetings where ways of destroying the church and promoting 'materialistic' and 'scientific' world outlooks were discussed. However, on Sundays, or at least major feast days, they would take part in a church service and profess their allegiance to God and Church. Higher Party officials could have church weddings, have their children baptized or sent for First Communion in secrecy. Their names were entered in special church registry books. There were even cases of double funerals – the official one with flags and the Internationale preceded by a quick church funeral. Even non-Party members were caught in this trap of double existence. To secure an untroubled life they would attend political rallies at their place of work, even the ones called specifically to denounce the Church. They would march on the Mayday workers' parade and shout socialist slogans while a few weeks later they would take part in a workers' pilgrimage to places of national spiritual focus such as Czestochowa or Piekary Slaskie and listen to sermons about the existing socialist system which enslaves the soul.

Even the national colours, restricted like the national anthem by the government unless officially ordered, reflect the dualism, for the Polish flag is red and white. A well-loved Polish poet who died in 1953 summed up popular feeling by this avowal. 'You will always be red and white, not white only, not red only.' And if white is taken to mean Christian, patriotic and free, and red to mean politically aware, concerned with human justice and human rights, then it would seem an ideal marriage. But the balance is not as nice, unfortunately. That the flag survives at all is a miracle, but too often in People's Poland the white has remained only at great expense, and the red almost submerged by the compulsion and administrative pressure which has been used to break the Church as the representative of Christian truth and the nation together.

That tension was reflected in the lives of children and young people growing up with the knowledge that double life was widely accepted as an unavoidable compromise. For in People's Poland schoolteachers taught one set of values to the children, and parents and the parish priest another. In comparison with young people in other Eastern European countries, those in Poland were relatively lucky, as members of a strong and independent church; but they were immensely frustrated because, even though they represented a Catholic majority, an atheist minority ruled them according to materialistic principles.

Various tactics, ranging from granting privileges to open blackmail, were used by the authorities to win over young Poles. If this failed they tried to break them spiritually.

Active membership in socialist youth associations would open any department of university to a young person; and to join the Party while studying would secure quick promotion and a prosperous life. In the ideological battle not even the youngest children were spared.

'Each June on the day of the Corpus Christi processions our school would arrange a special excursion,' recalls Grazyna Sikorska, a research worker at Keston College. 'One year, I remember, I was chosen to go on the excursion. It was a great honour, you know, a reward for being the best pupil.'

Grazyna was nine at the time. She had just made her first Holy Communion and badly wanted to please God and put on her white dress and walk in the Corpus Christi procession. But the excursion was very tempting too. She would be given a free ticket to an amusement park which was normally far too expensive for any of the children to visit. Besides, how could she refuse both the honour and the prize?

She asked her mother for help. 'You must make your own decision,' her mother said.

'It was terrible!' said Grazyna. 'I didn't know what to do.' She accepted the ticket, but in the end, on the day of the Corpus Christi procession of praise and worship, Grazyna was there with all the other children.

'I felt very liberated,' she recalls. 'It was a wonderful day. And on Monday the teacher asked me in front of the whole class how I had enjoyed my excursion. I handed back the ticket and told the teacher that I had preferred not to use it.'

Grazyna's singlemindedness then was to help her in her teenage years. Should she join the Party or not? If she didn't, no matter how good her marks were she wouldn't get a place in the university of her choice. After all, she could always sign up and then hand back the card afterwards. Everyone else did, even her priest told her so.

Grazyna didn't join the Party, and although she got a university place, it was only because, by lucky coincidence, the number of places on the course were doubled, as well as the fact that she received top marks in the entrance examination. But by then she was thoroughly disenchanted with a Church which seemed to her to offer no clear answers, surviving as it did because of popular support, but often at the cost of speaking, so it seemed to Grazyna, with a clear-cut decisive voice on the complex moral problems which drove many disillusioned young people in the sixties into a weary cynicism. What was the point of anything? many wondered, Grazyna included.

But during a summer vacation a friend persuaded Grazyna to go to a centre outside Warsaw where nuns care for blind and handicapped children, and there Grazyna saw Christianity in action.

'It's the most beautiful place in the whole church in Poland,' she declares warmly. 'Christian life is so evident there.'

To Grazyna's surprise there were many young people there, including a group of young Christians from East Germany, who came each year to atone for their country's part in the destruction of Poland during the war. And that alone spoke volumes.

Grazyña came to England in 1974, and then came back again to do research, and has now settled here.

But all the time a question was haunting her. How can I be true to myself? she wondered. The devoted, selfless caring of the nuns had aroused deep questions in her, showing her a dimension of Christianity she had never known before; one she had found reflected in the Life-Light renewal movement, which has transformed the lives of thousands of Polish Christians and about which Grazyna herself writes in *Religion in Communist Lands*:

> Under the conditions of official dechristianization the harsh reality was that only a person who could share his faith with others could keep it himself.

Even in post-war Poland the Church maintained three important focuses: the 'mass media' of the pulpit broke the monopoly of the State-controlled media; its network of religious instruction classes broke the educational monopoly of a government which aimed at total control over every branch of society; and, above all, the Church became a focus for truth where human rights were valued, spiritual freedom asserted and a feeling of individuality and 'Polishness' maintained.

It was not without an immense struggle. Every right, even the smallest, had to be fought for. What the State seemed to concede on the one hand it took away with the other, as the story of the Corpus Christi procession shows, and an able priest would find himself being carefully vetted and offered every inducement to compromise. The man whom we now know as Pope John Paul II was no exception. It happened that when Karol Wojtyla was Bishop of Krakow, as long ago as 1958, the authorities decided to take over a building which belonged to the Diocese of Krakow and was in use as a seminary. Bishop Wojtyla, transgressing all the accepted protocol of dealing only with government officials, appeared at the relevant Party office where the real power was and stunned the Party bureaucrat with his simple request: please rescind this unjust decision. The Party official, completely taken aback, telephoned Warsaw, to no less a person than Gomulka's second-in-command, Zenon Kliszko, who was equally amazed and asked the name of the enterprising, not to say, audacious young bishop. When in December 1963 Cardinal Wyszynski put forward to the government names of possible candidates for the vacant archbishop's post, Comrade Kliszko spotted a familiar surname and pointed it out as one worthy of confirmation by the Party! He thus indirectly contributed to Karol Wojtyla becoming the first Polish Pope. As one Polish Catholic intellectual commented: 'The ways of the Holy Spirit are mysterious indeed. He uses the most unexpected channels to accomplish His plans!' The new archbishop was at once offered advantageous prospects. Propaganda was bandied about in his favour, declaring him to be a progressive, an ardent ally of the new socialist reality, while Cardinal Wyszynski was said to be a narrow reactionary, quite out of touch with the modern world. But Archbishop Wojtyla trod a tactful but firm path past all Party blandishments, refusing to participate in any situation which might shed a favourable light on himself and an unfavourable one on the superior he so deeply respected.

As archbishop and then cardinal, Karol Wojtyla continued in the warm flexible ways the world has come to know so well. And, not surprisingly, the man who kept 'open house' in his episcopal palace, welcoming groups of 'non-people' banned by the authorities, actively supported the renewal movement which blossomed in the Church of the sixties and seventies, developing into a nation-wide phenomenon 50,000 strong.

This awakening was initially the work of a priest named Father Blachnicki, in the West since the imposition of martial law, who ran retreats for altar boys which grew into the 'Oasis' movement. The movement continues to be based on spiritual retreats where participants are helped to have an individual encounter with Christ, with 'Light and Life' parish groups meeting weekly for a gospel-based renewal of life. From these groups again emerged the concept of the Living Church: a Church whose life and strength is expressed by communities of believers building new lives together.

The whole thing literally 'took-off' in the mid seventies. Numbers mushroomed and the lives of people involved were absolutely transformed, becoming transparent with the light of Jesus, an immensely attractive and powerful witness to their faith, and characterized by the sort of maturity which comes when Christians are encouraged to live out their discipleship no matter what the consequences.

'I decided to witness to Christ at any time and place, under any circumstances,' declared one participant. 'At Oasis I discovered who Jesus really is and what a central role he can play in my life,' wrote another, 'I have learnt to love not only God but my neighbour as well.' 'I want Jesus' way to become my way,' concluded a third.

And that way is based firmly on an understanding of the cross. As Father Blachnicki himself writes:

> One must be able to overcome fear in order to bear testimony to and live by the light. Therefore the cross, in which we find the strength to overcome fear, is part of the Light-Life experience [Light-Life is the name by which the Oasis movement is now known] . . . A person is free when he has the courage to bear witness to the truth and to live by the truth regardless of any suffering and sacrifice. The Light-Life movement arose from the endeavour to live according to this principle.
>
> Everything that makes up the movement was from the very beginning forbidden and illegal in Poland . . . We simply followed the principles of never asking what we were allowed to do, but rather doing what we must do as Christians who want to live according to the gospel in the freedom of God's children. We never let fear keep us from doing what we felt we must do as disciples of Christ.

Bearing witness to the truth, as the Pope urged his fellow-countrymen and women, is what the Life-Light movement is all about. Grazyna herself has found that her work in Keston College enables her at last to be true to herself and to the homeland she is unable to visit now. She translates from her native language articles and documents and sermons, and rushes her translations, together with news of arrests and harassment, off to the Press, determined to resist the dualism which connives at pretence. She agrees strongly with Father Blachnicki:

It is the fact that we are forced to live in a permanent state of hypocrisy that is the real source, even the essence, of our captivity . . . This also means, however, that no one can deprive us of our freedom except ourselves. Christ, whether standing before Pilate or nailed to the cross, remained completely free, bearing witness to the truth that God is love.

In the very centre of the Solidarity revolution was the spiritual value of truth, a protest against falsehood. In the consciousness of the striking and struggling workers there was a deeply rooted, if not always clearly formulated, intuitive conviction that people are free when they witness to the truth they know and acknowledge. The Soviet system of enslavement, which is above all based on lies, awakened such a strong yearning for liberation by the truth that the example of the Gdansk workers' struggle for freedom quickly fired the entire nation to break the barriers of fear, which does not allow people to witness to the truth or to demand their rights. During the Solidarity period Poles recognized and experienced the way of liberation.

Then came 13 December 1981, the imposition of martial law, and the budding revolution was crushed by the use of force. Will the Polish authorities succeed in returning their country to its pre-revolutionary, pre-Solidarity condition? Will they succeed in blotting from the people's consciousness the way they found to liberation? Or, sadly, will a new generation grow up for whom the only reality is still a system of lies?

> When they took the worker
> From the building next door
> He said, 'History will never forgive you'
> But they didn't listen to him
> (The child standing on the stairs overheard)
> They put him in chains
> There were four of them and one of him
> Thousands of people brewed tea
> While the December snow fell.[6]

Thus the poet, but what about the children themselves, onlookers of their country's daily struggles, silent witnesses of the state of war?

If they take mummy and not me ... I will cry for my mummy. But perhaps they won't find us because there are many houses around where we live. (Renata aged 7)

Our teacher is a Party secretary. Nobody loves her or even likes her. In our class it happens that everyone's parents are in Solidarity. It was horrible to hear our teacher's threats, but then she just stopped shouting and burst into tears. (Janek aged 12)

If they arrest my sister I will take around the (underground) publications as she does, so help me God, whatever happens. I gave my sister 1,000 zlotys from my savings for the underground ... she took 500zl., but anyway I took the remaining 500 and put them into a box at St Martin's Church because they help the interned. A lady with Mother of God on a flag asked me if I hadn't taken the money from my parents and I said 'no' and she believed me. Now that my birthday is coming up I asked all my family to give me money so I will have something again. Only I asked my sister for a Mother of God on a flag or for a picture of Walesa. (Dorota aged 11)

I did not know that they had taken my father away. I was asleep with my brother and I did not hear a thing. Nothing at all. But my brother must have heard something because he was crying and mummy was trying to calm him down. He is very small. He can barely talk. Next day our neighbour burst into tears when she saw me. She said my dad was in prison for Solidarity. At first I was ashamed that my father was in prison because no one in our family has ever been in prison, and I remember that when the father of one of my classmates was put in prison for stealing the other boys laughed at him and called him 'the son of a thief'. At school the teacher gave me some sausage and some money. She said that the money was for us and the sausage was for my father. I told her then that my father was not in prison but was travelling. And I started to cry.

The teacher told me that I should not be ashamed because it is not my father who is guilty but the men who put him in prison. (Marek aged 10)

Costly though Poland's struggle for freedom is proving, it has profound implications for Christians in all the other Eastern European countries, not least its close neighbours, Catholic Slovakia and the Baltic State of Lithuania. The story of the Church in Lithuania is followed with great interest in Keston College and has been told by Michael Bourdeaux in *Land of Crosses*, a book which won him the honour of being made a Knight of Lithuania by the Lithuanian community in the USA. This is a story of people who have willingly given up their freedom for the right to believe, and it is closely linked with a longing for a national identity and language, but it is above all a story of heartfelt faith and conviction which neither persecution, nor prison, nor exile, nor death itself can destroy.

'Lord Jesus, you are my light in the darkness, you are my warmth in the cold. You are my happiness in sorrow.' So runs a prayer from four young Lithuanian girls in prison and in exile for their faith. And men in prison have been no less courageous:

They knelt facing the wall, crossed themselves and prayed for five to ten minutes. Before long we came to imitate them, because the example they gave made us blush with shame at not having the bravery to bear witness to our faith. Moreover, these brave country-folk openly wore their baptismal crosses on their necks, thus making a silent testimony to their belonging to Jesus Christ.[7]

But if the Lithuanian Christians are bold enough to stand up for their faith, encouraged by the Church in Poland, the police are plainly all the more harsh in their dealings with them. 'It all began with a rosary in Poland', one security man said darkly.

[1] *Religion in Communist Lands*, vol. 11, no. 1, spring 1983.
[2] Quoted in A. Tomsky, *Catholic Poland*. Keston College 1982.

[3] *Keston News Service*, no. 30, 23 September 1976.

[4] *Chronicle of the Lithuanian Catholic Church*, no. 49, 8 September 1981.

[5] Dmitri Dudko, *Our Hope*. St Vladimir's Seminary Press 1977.

[6] Te Jot, 'Mierzwa'; trans. by Jenny Robertson. Thanks are due to Puls Publications in whose *Poems on the State of War* (1984) the poem was originally published in Polish.

[7] Dmitri Panin, quoted in Michael Bourdeaux, *Land of Crosses*. Augustine Publishing Co. 1979.

6

'The university of life'

The crosses have gone up to heaven in smoke! Christ, our King, may your Kingdom come to our country.[1]

Only love makes everything easy.

Nijole Sadunaite

In Lithuania, despite the presence in the Vatican of a Polish Pope who is well aware of the plight of Christians there, severe repressions have not stopped short of the murder of priests and laity alike. As long ago as 1972 a group of priests spelt out the situation of the Church in their country:

Lithuania's Catholics have no catechisms, prayer books, church press or literature. The children of believing parents are in atheist schools. The seminary produces 4–6 priests every year, whereas 20–30 die each year. Priests are jailed merely because they dare to teach the truths of the faith at the request of parents. Priests are punished merely because children serve at Mass and participate in processions. Without trials, two bishops have been banished for over 10 years. Very active priests are hustled off to small parishes and elderly priests are sent to large ones.[2]

Cold facts are fleshed out in human experience and the following stories show how hard it is for active young Christians in Lithuania today.

As in other parts of the Soviet Union when young people are known to be believers they receive low marks at school no matter how good their work really is. They are often persecuted by security agents. 'There is no place you can escape from us! You will meet with us even if unwillingly,' one disabled student was told. He found himself confronted by security agents wherever he went. They asked for details of every friendship he was involved in until in the end he became scared to go out at all or mix with anyone.

On the other hand, a young man hoping to enter theological seminary may find himself being courteously greeted by the security police. 'We'll help you, you can help us; we'll get you into the seminary and you'll give us some bits of information . . .'[3]

It is thought that every ordained priest has been forced to undergo the 'ordeal by fire' which was experienced by one unsuccessful candidate to the seminary, Alesandras Gofmanas. As soon as he applied for a place at the seminary Alesandras received a visit at the clinic where he worked from a stranger who acted like an old friend, although, oddly enough, he carefully avoided contact with anyone else there.

'Come on outside with me and have a talk. It's urgent,' the man said.

Alesandras asked for a name and the man introduced himself as Antanas.

'I'll come with you, but I'll have a quick word with the boss first. He's got a right to know about this. After all, it's a working day,' Alesandras pointed out.

'No, no, don't do that. No one must know anything about this. There's no need to tell your boss every little thing, is there? Well, if you feel like that we'll postpone our chat until you're free. How about tomorrow?'

'I'm on afternoon shift tomorrow,'Alesandras said.

'Then would 9 a.m. suit you? We'll meet in Lenin Square. Wait for me on one of the benches beside the Lenin monument. But remember, no one must know, absolutely no one at all. O.K.?'

Alesandras met the agent who took him into a darkened room, turned the radio up and began to question him about his future plans, until Alesandras was forced to admit that he had a vocation for the priesthood and had applied to the theological seminary for a place.

'The seminary, eh? It's very hard to get in, you know. There are all sorts of tests before they let you in, but if I were to put in a good word for you you'd certainly be accepted. How about that now?'

'No thanks. I don't need your help,' Alesandras replied.

'Oh, come now, a fine young lad like you! You're the very sort we want to see get in: honest, truthful, conscientious, hard-working. I've got an eye for character. I've noticed a thing or two about you. Look, we must meet again.'

The agent tried phoning Alesandras at work. In the end Alesandras put the phone down, cutting off the agent.

'Naturally,' wrote Alesandras in a letter detailing this experience, 'I was not admitted to the seminary.'

He sent a copy of his letter to the Catholic Committee for the Defence of Believers' rights, another to the Principal of Kaunas seminary and a third to the *Chronicle of the Lithuanian Catholic Church* which since 1972 has circulated among Lithuanians in *samizdat* form. Typed and produced at great risk, the *Chronicle* details the life of the Church today and is often as dramatic and thrilling as the records of the early Church. The following account of the trial of Gemma Stanelyte taken from the *Chronicle*[4] gives a flavour of this remarkable unofficial paper. Gemma, an active Christian who had finally been forced to give up her job, had led pilgrimages and religious processions which were as much part of Lithuania's cultural as well as religious life.

On 16 December 1980 in Kelme the trial of Gemma-Jadvyga Stanelyte took place. The security police wanted this trial to be held without anyone knowing it: even her nearest relatives were not informed. Early in the morning, while it was still dark, a group of Gemma's friends met at the doors of the court-house. When a grey prisoner van pulled up before the court-house and a gap appeared in the line of militia one of Gemma's friends jumped to the steel prison van and cried loudly right at the crack between the doors of the van, 'Gemma! Little Gemma! We're with you!'

Gemma-Jadvyga Stanelyte was accused under article 240 of parasitism and under article 199.3d of disturbing the peace.

Defendant Stanelyte boldly proclaimed she had organized and partially led the procession because old Lithuanian customs were dear to her . . . if the procession had not been religious it would not have bothered anyone.

In her final statement Miss Stanelyte said, 'I am deeply religious. Even though freedom is precious my religion is more valuable to me than freedom.'

During the trial, even though the weather was cold and damp, nevertheless the crowd outside did not disperse, but steadily grew and grew. Those passing by asked what sort of criminal was being tried, and learning that she was being tried for religion and for a procession to Siluva [a centre of popular devotion] they did not want to believe it, and many would remain standing about, wishing to see how it would all end. Those who had come from afar, sleepless, hungry and stiff from the cold, stood the whole day on the street. Even though towards evening it began to rain, they did not disperse.

When the trial was over and the prison van had driven out on the street the crowd began to toss flowers on to the vehicle, crying out, 'Gemma! We love you! Gemma! We love you!'

Gemma Stanelyte is a good friend of someone who must be one of the most courageous and radiant Christians not only of the persecuted church, but of the church as a whole: Nijole Sadunaite.

Nijole's story is told in the *Chronicle of the Lithuanian Catholic Church*, a copy of which was found in her typewriter at her arrest on 27 May 1974. Michael Bourdeaux gives us two portraits of her in *Land of Crosses* and *Risen Indeed* and her autobiography has reached friends in the USA.

Born in 1939, Nijole has allowed persecution, threats, starvation, thirst, hunger, hard labour, mockery, deprivation and constant physical weakness, the result of harsh penal conditions, to hone her to an almost transparent radiance, flooded through and through with a very special saintliness, a total unselfishness rooted in love.

To hard-bitten security agents, soldiers, police and hostile atheists Nijole declared at her trial:

I'd like to tell you all that I love you as if you were my own brothers and sisters and I wouldn't hesitate to give my life for each one of you . . . I'm being tried because I love our people and desire the truth. Loving men is the greatest love and fighting for their rights is the most beautiful love-song. May it echo in everyone's hearts and never stop! I'm privileged, my fate is an honourable one: not only have I fought for human rights and justice, but I'm being punished for doing so. My sentence will be my triumph . . . How can I fail to be happy when Almighty God has shown that light triumphs over lies and falsehood! In order to bring this about I'm willing not only to be imprisoned but also to die.

So let's love one another and we'll be happy . . . only love makes everything seem easy! We have to condemn evil as harshly as possible, but we must love men, even if they are wrong. And we can learn to do this in the school of Jesus Christ, who is our Way, our Truth and our Life. May your kingdom, Jesus, come into every soul!

I have one last request of this court: free all prisoners and all those who have been taken to psychiatric hospitals for human rights and justice. You'd thus show your good-will and it would be a good beginning toward a new and better life, so that your beautiful motto, 'A man is brother to his fellow man' would become a reality.[5]

Nijole herself was frequently threatened with admission to psychiatric hospital in the nine months of her imprisonment awaiting trial. For two months she was denied any food parcels from outside, a hint of the deprivations which would follow.

The amazing strength of her defence speech, which she conducted without a lawyer, proclaiming fearlessly the dearly held truths for which she was glad to sacrifice her freedom, was surely built up in the bitter months before her trial during which she resolutely maintained silence in the face of hunger and uncertainty, refusing to be manipulated by outright bullying.

After her trial she was transported to Mordovia. She was herded with women criminal prisoners into a variety of cells, often underground, usually filthy and damp and always so insanitary that her health worsened; but she was refused any

61

medication. She endured journeys by train, locked in iron cages through the heat of a continental summer and received only bread, salt fish and water. Nijole took only the water, and of this month-long trial wrote:

> ... all the romance of a journey which is indescribable, for one has to undergo it oneself to be able to experience life and understand the need and value of love ... How good it is that the small craft of my life is being steered by the hand of the good Father. When he is at the helm nothing is to be feared. Then, no matter how difficult life may be, you will know how to resist and love.

After her arduous journey Nijole was too weak to endure the unhygienic conditions in glass-cutting workshops and was made to sew gloves instead: seventy pairs a day whether the machines worked or not.

> The work is oppressive in its monotony and frequent mechanical defects add to this—patience is needed ... but the norm does not wait for us ... I complete my norm because we work in a single shift. I can begin sewing at 6 a.m. and finish at 10 p.m. In this way everything is going excellently at present. Everyone likes me and I try to return their kindness. I am fortunate and contented.

Of the slave labour provided by women prisoners one Orthodox believer Yuliya Voznesenskaya wrote:

> During three years in exile, in prison and in camps I had met thousands of women deprived of freedom. Their fates were so tragic that even today I cannot begin to speak of them without pain in my heart. First of all I was convinced that the existence of camps for women was dictated above all not by a growth in female criminality in a 'country of triumphant socialism', but simply by the State's practical need for an unpaid work-force: for example the entire Soviet army has shoes made almost exclusively by women prisoners. And the most terrible thing is that any attempt to appeal to the law is useless—the law is on the side of the slave-owning State.[6]

But Nijole, a prisoner-slave, writes: 'I rejoice that I have been brought here in accordance with my calling—to nurse and to love.'

In 1977 Nijole's prison sentence finished. She then had to endure a month in prison waggons transported from Mordovia to Siberia in such unhygienic conditions that her health broke completely: 'On 5 September,' writes Nijole, 'I almost journeyed to the place where there is no pain and no tears—what was most interesting was that I felt quite calm—no fear. I had only one clear thought: thank God, everything is ending.'

Weakened, deaf in one ear, penniless, so that she would have starved without 'the sparks of goodness in people's souls', Nijole was set to work scrubbing floors in the local school, but a chronic inflammation of the gall bladder sent her to hospital, thus saving her deportation to a notorious state farm so remote that it could only be reached by the plane which calls there three days a week. The authorities wanted to deport her because friends from Lithuania had managed to visit her in the Siberian village. Her ill-health thwarted their plans.

She was set free on 8 July 1980 and was flown to Vilnius, her home city, via Riga in Latvia. However, her persecution was by no means over. Secret security agents met the plane in Riga and Nijole was driven by car the rest of the way, a five-hour journey. This was done so that the people who had gathered at the airport both in Riga and Vilnius couldn't greet her with the flowers they had brought for her, but all the same the news of her return soon got about. People crowded to see her and those who met her said, 'Thank you, Nijole, for your love and sacrifice.' And Nijole would reply, 'Thank you, thank you all for your prayers and support. It was only thanks to your prayers that I was able to bear it all.'[7]

Nijole had been greatly helped during her time in prison and exile by the knowledge that her friends had sent letters, even though the actual mail was often withheld from her. Now she is unable to receive any letters from friends abroad. Parcels have been returned and Nijole's own letters to Gemma Stanelyte didn't reach Gemma.

Nijole is still taking an active part in the life and worship of the persecuted church, so further punishment undoubtedly awaits her, part of the 'university of life' as she calls it, which taught her the depths of cruelty and the heights of goodness. Of her persecutors Nijole has written: 'Nothing now amazes me; it only remains for me to pray for them.' And of Nijole herself her persecutors are plainly in awe. Her example has made her fellow-believers who are brought to trial declare themselves proud to stand where Nijole has stood, but the KGB agents, trying to silence them, say grimly, 'We don't want to make a Sadunaite out of you!'

Nijole's moving description of a fellow-prisoner, a young Orthodox girl, gives us an insight into her own character:

> Five years of punishment cell and strict-regime prison with hardly a break—starvation, cold and ridicule. She is a true heroine before whom we should all kneel. Quiet, calm, always smiling, with a prayer on her lips. I never heard her utter an impatient or rough word. She goes to the punishment cell smiling and returns smiling. Exhausted, blue with cold, she looks terrible yet smiles not only at us but at her tormentors as well.

Nijole herself radiates exactly this same courage, prayerfulness and joy. No wonder Michael Bourdeaux has written of her: 'any single day of her life over the last ten years marks her out for future sainthood in her church.'

Lithuania itself is a small country, tucked away on the fringes of Europe, and for the last four decades almost engulfed by the enormous might of the Soviet Union which has stamped its language as well as its policies on the life of the conquered nation. None the less, although very few outsiders ever actually study Lithuanian, that language survives in its homeland, and *émigré* groups in Britain, America and elsewhere have kept their language alive. For example, I myself visited a crumbling tenement in the bulldozed Gorbals district of Glasgow where a Lithuanian grandad proudly displayed books with which he taught Lithuanian to generations of his community's children. Sadly, his wife was in hospital and no one could be found who could speak Lithuanian to a confused old lady who was forgetting her English.

There are no Lithuanians on the staff of Keston College, but one of the research workers with the team comes from a Latvian family and also reads Lithuanian. Marite Sapiets spent part of her childhood in Edinburgh where her father, a good friend to Keston College, was pastor to the Latvian Lutheran congregation while working at the same time in a Scottish Presbyterian congregation. She speaks Latvian, Russian and Czech, having spent a year in Prague in 1969, a difficult time for a foreigner who had been sent there to learn Russian. People were hostile and suspicious if addressed in Russian and she had to fall back on English for a while.

Latvia too is now part of the Soviet Union, but its history is different from neighbouring Lithuania. Latvia has only one region with a strong Catholic tradition, the Lutheran Church being the main Church of the country.

'Latvians are probably more pragmatic and less deeply religious than the Lithuanians,' Marite says, and recalls stories heard in her childhood of remnants of paganism surviving in rural areas. 'It's probably wiped out now by collectivization, but Hallowe'en, Velunakts, it was called, used to be celebrated in some remote parts. The oldest male in the household would sit up after the family had gone to bed, ready to play host to any visiting dead who would come to partake of various traditional dishes which were set out on the table.' Presumably the weary host would end his vigil with a solitary feast. There's food for the story-teller there!

One of Marite's own special interests is the Seventh Day Adventists in the USSR and she is completing a book about this much persecuted Church. She is also interested in *samizdat*, the illegal self-published material which is the only outlet for many Christian writers and thinkers in the Soviet Union, and has translated into English a *samizdat* novel, *The Unknown Homeland*, the true story of a Russian priest at the time of the Revolution who dies in Siberian exile. Included in the *samizdat*, of course, are numbers of the *Chronicle of the Lithuanian Catholic Church*, copies of which regularly reach Keston, showing how highly the persecuted Church values contact with an organization which can make its voice heard. The *samizdat Chronicle* in its turn provides vital information about a Church surviving against all the odds, restricted, unable to innovate, be 'trendy' or simply 'move with the times', which none the less attracts children and young people who throw away their job prospects, their freedom and even, in some tragic cases, their lives.

Lithuanian Catholics feel a special sympathy for members of the Eastern-Rite Catholic Church[8] which was once a feature of church life in Ukraine and elsewhere. The Church was totally banned in 1946. Its bishops were all arrested and the priests either forced into the Orthodox Church or imprisoned for a minimum of ten years. The Church survives secretly and some priests actually go into Lithuania and work as labourers but try to organize church activity from there, undoubtedly at great personal risk.

Particularly tragic is the story of a young Ukrainian Christian called Vitali who, realizing he had a vocation for the priesthood in the banned Eastern-Rite Church, came as an enterprising 15-year-old to Vilnius to learn Lithuanian in order eventually to enter theological seminary. He became actively involved in the life of the Lithuanian Catholic Church, was interrogated repeatedly by the KGB who tried to persuade him to become one of their agents, promising to get him into seminary without having to do military service first. Soon after his eighteenth birthday Vitali was found dead in his room, his face battered in.[9]

The Eastern-Rite Church is banned in Romania too. Officially it is said that this branch of the Church was voluntarily merged with the Orthodox Church in 1948. In fact, coercion and pressure ensured that a small number of clergy did press for the union; the rest as in Ukraine went underground.

A second banned religious group in Romania also carries on in secret and is harshly punished. Called the Lord's Army, this is a lay-centred revival movement within the Orthodox Church. As the Oasis movement in Poland has recognized, when Christians enter the full realization of all that commitment to Christ implies, renewal follows which is attractive and contagious. So the Lord's Army, despite appalling persecution and despite the attempts of the State to seize control of the whole Church, continues to vitalize Orthodoxy in

Romania, attracting some of the best priests and many lay-people.

Although officially there are good relationships between the Churches and the State, and the number of Christians, particularly Protestants, is increasing, in fact repression is as severe in Romania as anywhere else in Eastern Europe. Josif Ton, the Baptist leader, an energetic, vigorous figure and a notable theologian, is in exile in the West, while the regime's persecution of one of the bravest and most dedicated Ortho-dox priests, Father Gheorghe Calciu-Dumitreasa, casts a doubtful light on any suggestion of real religious freedom under President Ceausescu and his government.

Father Calciu was ordained at the age of fifty-one in 1973 and was appointed to a teaching post in French and New Testament studies at the Orthodox seminary in Bucharest where he quickly gained a reputation for forceful and inspir-ing teaching. Like Nijole, Father Calciu has learnt deeply in 'the university of life', and for him too this has included years in prison. In the Stalinist era Gheorghe was held in a notorious prison, Pitesti, where experiments were made to brainwash tortured prisoners into becoming torturers. Facts about this began to leak out, but the authorities, forced to admit the brutalities, put out that they were manipulated by fascist influence. Gheorghe denied this and was condemned to fifteen more years in prison. His sense of vocation to the priesthood came (like Frantisek Lizna's) in prison. In Father Calciu's case it was an act of gratitude for his very survival.

His concern for truth and justice and the right to believe has brought upon Father Calciu torture, beatings and inter-rogation for days on end while deprived of food and sleep. His life is now in danger in prison, but despite world-wide pressure the government refuses to release a man who is already a living martyr. One recent report indicated that his hands were beaten because he was caught praying.

Father Calciu had joined the Committee for the Defence of Religious Freedom, a movement which had its origins among the Baptists. He preached in the patriarchal cathedral on 30 January 1978, publicly denouncing atheism as a 'philo-sophy of despair'. Church officials were quick to reprimand him and forbid him to preach in the cathedral again, but

Father Calciu continued to speak openly about the problems of a Church forced to be infiltrated by an atheistic state. He attracted a large following among the students, despite frantic attempts by their professors to keep them away. On one occasion (according to the Committee for the Defence of Religious Freedom) students were locked in their dormitories to stop them going to hear Father Calciu's sermons. And evening prayers were cancelled completely more than once.

In May 1978 the church authorities suspended Father Calciu from the staff of the theological college and transferred him to an administrative post. The Committee for the Defence of Religious Freedom, fearing that he might fall into the hands of the Romanian Secret Police, appealed to the Patriarch to recognize Gheorghe Calciu's spiritual value and take up his cause, but in March 1979 Father Calciu was placed under arrest and suffered beatings and ill-treatment in order to extort a confession, while other members of the Committee were kept under constant surveillance, threatened and questioned.

Reports conflicted whether Father Calciu was being kept in prison or psychiatric hospital. Mrs Calciu herself knew nothing, but understood that charges of 'parasitism' were to be brought against her husband—unless he agreed to emigrate, which he refused to do. A newspaper editorial linking the human rights movement with fascist ideology made Gheorghe's friends fear that serious charges were pending, and an eye-witness account declaring that he was being interrogated continuously, deprived of sleep and food, increased everyone's fears.

The Paris paper *Le Monde* reported on 12 April 1979 that a Romanian priest had been accused of being a fascist. Keston College received an alarming document through the post in which five of Father Calciu's fellow-priests alleged that he had been a fascist all through his career and claimed that there was complete religious freedom in Romania, giving statistics to prove it. In July 1979 Father Gheorghe Calciu was sentenced to ten years in prison.

Why do good men remain silent? Do you free men of the Western world continue to look only to your own affairs?

. . . You were enthusiastic to see man place his feet on the moon, but you do not know how to plead for your brothers. We have been chosen for captivity and suffering, we who were born, live and remain here. But we want you to feel for us in our suffering and cry out when we cannot: 'Enough!'[10]

These searing words from a tortured man are alone enough to justify Keston's involvement in the trials and sufferings of those 'chosen for captivity' for their beliefs. Michael Bourdeaux feels very closely bound to Gheorghe Calciu whom he has been privileged to meet. Shortly before Father Calciu's arrest Michael was invited with his two children Karen and Mark to Romania. They were given red carpet treatment, but 11-year-old Mark gave himself the job of 'sussing out propaganda' and indeed proved remarkably good at it! On one occasion at dinner Mark successfully diverted the guide's attention so that Michael was able to slip away unobserved for a secret meeting with Father Calciu. It must have meant a great deal to Father Calciu on the eve of his arrest to know that, even though he was silenced, the story of his fate was being told beyond the boundaries of his own country. It is thanks to Michael's own willingness to give up his parish, his livelihood and security, in obedience to that vision of the suffering church which had come to him in the quiet Moscow room years before, that Gheorghe Calciu has found a voice to relay his tragedy to the wider world.

Amnesty International has appealed to the Romanian government for the release of Father Calciu, but when in September 1981 Romania, seeking favourable trade terms with the USA and hoping for backing for a grant from the IMF, released Christian prisoners, Father Calciu was not among them.

Ill, emaciated, fighting for his life, possibly blind, and with five gruelling years still to serve, Father Calciu can no longer cry 'enough', but in an English village outside London a team of workers has taken up his cry.

In a situation of fear and repression in which anti-religious ideology is being propagated even more insistently in the USSR, when will Christians who are free learn to plead for our brothers and sisters? Alas, too often we leave them, silenced and bound—running a race with both legs tied, as Aida so vividly describes. So often, if they plead, they must do so themselves, even for years on end, as one indomitable Pentecostal family unitedly, repeatedly and finally successfully did. The fight for freedom by the people known now world-wide as the Siberian Seven is carefully recorded in the files of Keston College. It will tax the short space of the next chapter to narrate just a small part of it.

[1] Quoted in Michael Bourdeaux, *Land of Crosses*. Augustine Publishing Co. 1979.

[2] *Religion in Communist Lands*, vol. 1, nos. 4–5, July–October 1973; text also in *The Tablet*, 6 January 1973.

[3] *Chronicle of the Lithuanian Catholic Church*, no. 43, June 1980.

[4] *Chronicle*, no. 46, December 1980.

[5] Michael Bourdeaux tells Nijole's story in *Risen Indeed* (Darton, Longman and Todd 1983) and *Land of Crosses* (see n. 1 above) where he gives a fuller account of her trial.

[6] Yuliya Voznesenskaya, 'The Independent Women's Movement in Russia', *RCL*, vol. 10, no. 3, winter 1982.

[7]. *Chronicle*, no. 44, July 1980.

[8] Eastern-Rite Catholicism was a historic compromise between the Catholic and Orthodox Churches. Part of the Orthodox Church in Ukraine accepted the supreme authority of the Pope, thus becoming Catholic while keeping the Orthodox liturgy and other Orthodox traditions.

[9] *Chronicle*, no. 17, July 1975; quoted in *Land of Crosses* (see n. 1 above).

[10] *Keston News Service*, no. 73, 24 May 1979.

7

'Ten minutes is enough!'

My persecutors, I do not curse you . . . I pray for you and
bless you with the simple humanity of Christ.

Georgi Vins

Hundreds of appeals, and numerous visits to Moscow with
requests to many different bodies were made by us; two
hunger strikes and three demonstrations in Chernogorsk,
Krasnoyarsk and Moscow give witness to the fact that you
took us captive, have held us fast and refused to let us go.

Letter from the Vashchenko family to Andropov,
18 January 1983

One of the groups of believers for whom persecution has
been virtually unbroken for over fifty years are the Soviet
Pentecostals, many of whom cannot see any hope for themselves or their families in the land of their birth. Thousands
of families have applied to emigrate but have mostly been
completely unsuccessful in being allowed to do so. As early
as 1963 a group of thirty-two Pentecostals travelled from
Chernogorsk in Siberia to Moscow, a journey of about 4000
kilometres. They rushed into the American Embassy, taking
Soviet guards by surprise and asked to be allowed to emigrate. Among them were the parents of the Vashchenko
family, who had in fact tried unsuccessfully to get into the
embassy the year before. American officials insisted that
there was nothing they could do immediately and told the
group to leave. Soviet officials promised that there would be
no retaliation and indeed agreed that a commission would
investigate the group's complaints about persecution. And
for a while the situation eased in Chernogorsk at least.

A long silence followed until, some eleven years later,
documents reached Keston from two different groups of Pen-

tecostal believers two thousand miles apart, appealing in joint letters for permission to emigrate to Israel, 'or some other country which doesn't deny the existence of God'. 'We do not have the right or possibility of being true believers in our country,' the letters said. 'We cannot educate our children in a religious spirit, or preach the gospel to others. We do not have Christian literature, Bibles, hymn books.'[1]

Then in 1976 the emigration movement began to take off. More appeals for mass emigration came into the archives of Keston College. The latter part of the decade saw a worsening situation for Christians. Pastors received heavy sentences. Threats and harsh fines brought hardship to families. Children were mocked and slandered at school and even removed from home simply because their parents were believers. As long ago as 1962 in answer to their requests for a Christian teacher the Vashchenko family were told, 'It would be better to let you leave the country than give you a Christian teacher.' Mothers feared the doctors in maternity hospitals. 'Who needs your children?' they were told. 'Why do you bring them into the world? Why do you breed poverty?' And Christian women in labour were frequently told, 'Let God help you.'

Neatly typed on strips of sheet, carefully sewn in six batches, came appeals from the Siberian mining town, Chernogorsk, where the Vashchenkos lived.

> Sirs, for the sake of God and of our Lord Jesus Christ, we beg and implore you to help us to emigrate from the Soviet Union. Oh, if only you knew how tired we are of the so-called humaneness of which the Soviet government loves to speak.[2]

As this chapter unfolds, the poignancy of that remark will become apparent. For it is against a background of extreme persecution that fresh appeals came to Keston College, and now Orthodox names add Christian solidarity to the Pentecostals' request to emigrate, 'in order to live where people serve God freely'.

Alexander Ginzburg, a well-known dissident, compiled documents for the Helsinki Monitoring Group, among which was a dossier of 343 closely typed pages, now in the Keston archives. The documents give details of 600 Pentecostals, including children, who wished to emigrate. Alexander Ginzburg commented: 'Both learned and unlearned minds are awakening from ignominious terror and are rocking a Russia which today lies enslaved.'

As the campaign to emigrate gained momentum the authorities promised some believers better housing and educational opportunities. Others, however, were threatened with reprisals. The pattern of crippling fines, arrests, harsh sentences continued unchanged. Finally, on 27 June 1978, the whole story hit the headlines of the world when seven members of two families from Chernogorsk, the Vashchenkos and the Chmykhalovs, successfully dashed into the American Embassy in Moscow, requesting to emigrate.

The Vashchenkos were already known to Keston. They had been involved in the unsuccessful 1963 attempt to get into the embassy and already the Keston archives contained letters and appeals from the family whose parents and thirteen children had experienced years of persecution. The authorities had long ago threatened to take the three eldest children away. Pyotr Vashchenko, the father, built a hiding place inside the house. Whenever the children played, one of them was always posted as sentry, on the look out for the KGB. One day, however, the 'sentry' became too absorbed in the game to notice the approach of the security police. Too late the children fled into their hiding place, but the eldest girl, Lida, around whom this story will centre, didn't have enough time to reach it. She hid in a shed but her foot was still sticking out. The KGB men grabbed hold of it and pulled her out. She was carried off. A month later two of her sisters were caught too.

The parents were deprived of their parental rights and were not even told where their three eldest daughters had been taken. They wrote to sixteen different educational authorities throughout the Soviet republics in an effort to trace their children. For six weeks there was no contact whatsoever, but eventually the girls managed to get word to their parents, thanks to the kindness of one of the cooks who wrote a letter for them. The parents came immediately. At first their visits took place in total secrecy, but the whole atmosphere in the institution was so deprived that later the staff were glad to turn a blind eye to the visits. In the course of time pressures eased a little and the visits became official, but the girls had to remain in the institution, being 're-educated' as Lida explained in an appeal later.

Lida was released when she was sixteen. A year later, in 1968, she was forced to take charge of the whole family as both her parents were arrested. Trying once again to gain admittance to the American Embassy Pyotr Vashchenko and his wife Augustina were arrested separately by the guards. Pyotr was put into psychiatric hospital, given drugs and sentenced to a year in prison. Augustina was sentenced to three years (even though she had small children at home). The authorities claimed she had bitten a militiaman and she was charged with hooliganism. When she arrived at the labour camp to serve her sentence the commandant burst out laughing when he read the charge sheet. 'You, bite a militiaman?' he exclaimed. She was eventually given a conditional discharge and transferred to a construction project where Pyotr was allowed to visit her. Soon afterwards Augustina discovered she was pregnant again and so was released.

Those were hard days for the family, and in particular for Lida. It was she who had to visit her parents in both their prisons. As it happened the dates coincided and Lida had to cut her visit to her father short in order to fit in her visit to her mother. The camp officials were shocked to discover that both parents had been arrested together.

After her release from the state institution Lida worked at various jobs, one of them being auxiliary nursing in the local maternity hospital. When she was twenty-four the chance came for her to adopt an unwanted baby boy whose mother had aborted him when she was seven months' pregnant. Lida was still single. The family vowed never to marry as long as they stayed on Soviet soil. Under Soviet law permission to emigrate must be sought from one's parents, no matter if the applicant is an adult. The Vashchenko family was fighting single-handed against the might of the Soviet state. They couldn't afford any complications from in-laws who could easily be pressured by the State and prevent even one family member from emigrating. Their commitment to one another was total.

The hospital authorities allowed Lida to adopt the child and all the relevant papers were signed, with the mother giving up her rights, but to Lida's dismay she was then refused permission to take the child home, and the treatment he was receiving caused her grave concern.

'I could see that he was perfectly healthy, but they kept on giving him injections,' Lida reported. Fearing for his life, she took him home where he quickly put on weight. Lida called him Aaron. Once the Town Council realized that Aaron now belonged to believers they did all they could to get him back, finally bringing the mother under police escort, even though she had signed away her rights. (Later the family learnt that she had been given a room in a hostel in return for her help.) The family protested. Lida produced her documents, but the police resorted to force. They broke in violently, pulling an entire window out, frame, glass and all. They beat Lida up and took Aaron away.

Now it was Lida's turn to search through one local authority building after another, but when she finally received news of her adopted son, it was to learn of his death.

'They took him from us on 17 July 1975,' wrote Lida in an appeal to the United Nations, 'and on 24 August he died at their hands.'

The family found where Aaron's grave was and learnt that the grave-diggers had not wanted to bury a child without any documents but were ordered to go ahead. 'The child was in a terrible mess. Unrecognizable. They told the grave-diggers that they had found his body in a field outside the town,' reported Lida.

The Vashchenkos dug up the coffin and took it home to open it. Then they photographed what they saw. That set of photographs is at Keston College now, and they are horrifying. Aaron had obviously been experimented on and had died as a result of the treatment he had received.

The family gave Aaron a Christian burial and Lida wrote a full report of the whole episode for the United Nations. 'We consider this to be murder and discrimination against believers in the Soviet Union,' she wrote. 'The child was legally mine. He couldn't go back to his natural mother so the only way out was to murder him.' She concluded, 'This appeal is in no way intended to arouse anyone's anger against the persecutors of the Church of Christ. God will require at their hands all the innocent blood which has been shed in the Soviet land.' Indeed, when the Vashchenko family finally won their long struggle and emigrated, Western reporters found them amazingly unhostile towards the regime they had struggled so long against.

Michael Rowe, a research worker at Keston College, met the Vashchenkos eighteen months after their sit-in began in the American Embassy and made their cause his own. He reports that the young Vashchenkos show a 'quiet faith and a total lack of bitterness'.

Mike, as he is known at Keston, to avoid confusion with Michael Bourdeaux, studied in Cambridge and then in Glasgow, at the Institute of Soviet Studies. Here he met Michael then in the early days of his work and still struggling to find finance and support. Mike caught Michael's vision and soon joined the team. He specializes in the study of Soviet evangelicals with his own typical quiet thoroughness.

Mike became familiar with the Vashchenko family's story. His close involvement began when he was asked to give an interview on *The World at One* the day after the Siberian Seven arrived at the embassy. 'They had hit the headlines, but Keston had background material in the archives. We knew the names, the dates of birth and we had their earliest appeals,' Mike explains. 'So we had information to give. The interview had the effect of making our archives and documents come alive.'

Eighteen months later Mike was in Moscow for a Baptist Congress and the chance came to snatch a ten-minute talk with the families, who were at that time kept very much in isolation.

Mike's meeting took place outside in the embassy yard in snow and slush and enabled him to form some clear impressions of the families. He realized that the very act of shutting the families up in the basement had reinforced their solidarity and determination. There could be no going back, and they had the inner resources, together with first-hand acquaintance of oppression, to be able to sit it out success-fully for a long time—though just how long it would be no one then quite foresaw.

Lida, Lyuba and their younger sister Lilia, fifth in the family, were there. Mike was struck by their quick thinking and intelligence. The brief meeting deepened Mike's involve-ment. From now on he followed the whole story even more closely; indeed he became part of it. When *Buzz* magazine launched a campaign to free the families in spring 1981 Mike became a close advisor of the campaign organizer Danny Smith. Mike and Danny kept in regular contact with the families in the embassy by means of telephone calls, which were of great value to Lida, especially when, weakened by a five-week hunger strike, she finally consented, at the end of January 1982, to be taken by the American authorities to hospital.

It was an act of great courage for Lida to agree to go alone into the unknown, putting herself at the mercy of the Soviet authorities. She had Aaron's sad story, as well as memories of her own kidnapping as a child, to make her distrust the authorities; indeed, the Vashchenkos made it a rule never to go anywhere alone, and especially never to Soviet official-dom. But Lida's consent marked a turning point, and although the media in this country portrayed it as a defeat, Mike saw it as a chance for the Soviet authorities to bring about a solution at last. (The Soviet government had always told the families that a solution would be found only if they left the embassy, went home and applied again from Cher-nogorsk.) Accordingly, Mike asked Danny to buy an air ticket for Lida valid for the capital of any of the European countries which had offered to take her. No one knew what would happen, but if the Soviets agreed to let Lida go the ticket at least was there.

However, once Lida was strong enough she agreed to go home to Chernogorsk again, to look after her younger broth-ers and sisters who at one point, after being placed under siege by the police, were forced to scavenge for food secretly. But her contact with Keston College continued. She man-aged to phone Mike from the post office at Chernogorsk. Things at that time seemed very uncertain. The authorities had just turned down her latest application to emigrate. Even so, Lida was sure she had done the right thing in leaving the embassy. 'Nothing seems to have changed,' she said over the phone, 'but I believe everything has changed. Mike, what do you think?'

And Lida was right. Her parents were still in the embassy and her mother continued her hunger strike, even when her life seemed threatened. 'I cannot think I can live very long,' she said. 'This is the last thing I can do for my children.' Lady Coggan, whose husband, Donald, Archbishop of Canterbury until his retirement in 1980, has always been a staunch supporter of the persecuted church and of Keston College, asked for prayers for the Siberian Seven. Many Christians responded, including Eric Dando, the secretary of the World Pentecostal Conference who died soon after Lida emigrated to the West.

March and April 1983 were decisive months for the waiting families when hope turned to decision. After twenty-two years of stalling and blocking, the authorities moved quickly and efficiently. On 23 March Lida was given forms to fill in for visas for either West Germany or Israel.

'Look, where it says what are my reasons for wishing to leave the Soviet Union, what shall I put?' she asked.

'Put the reason why you want to go,' she was told.

So Lida wrote carefully (and officially) 'on religious grounds', and that was written on her visa too.

Less than two weeks later she was called back to the visa office. 'You must collect your visa in Krasnoyarsk tomorrow, and then go to Moscow,' she was told by officials who were plainly totally dumbfounded by the sudden turn of events. Their utter incomprehension convinced Lida that it was all for real, and that they weren't playing a game. They handed her an air ticket to Krasnoyarsk and another to Moscow. 'This ticket has been paid for by the Central Committee of the Communist Party,' she was told.

'They didn't dare to be nasty!' Lida told Mike afterwards in Vienna. 'In fact I got VIP treatment! It all took place so quickly that it seemed to be happening to someone else.'

She still couldn't be sure that the authorities would allow the rest of her family to leave too, but she knew for certain that she must take this big step and go on alone, trusting that the others would soon be following her. Just the same, they still couldn't be absolutely sure, and since they never went anywhere alone Lida took her brother and sister, Ioann and Vera, with her. They took the overnight train to Krasnoyarsk that very night and there officials obtained two more air tickets to Moscow. Once in the capital Lida had no time to call at the embassy to say good-bye to her parents. She stayed at a friend's flat, collected an Austrian visa and her air ticket—the ticket bought for her fourteen months earlier—and travelled out to Moscow's Sheremetyevo airport. There she was thoroughly searched at Customs and the family's latest appeal to Andropov was found and confiscated. Then it was time for Lida to step out on to the tarmac and go alone up the steps of a plane bound for Vienna, still not knowing whether the step she was taking was going to separate her from her family for ever. Even yet she could hardly believe it was happening! In Vienna Lida was whisked away by Austrian officials through the VIP lounge, but Mike caught up with her in her hotel room, standing in her stockinged feet.

'Hullo,' he said. 'I'd forgotten how small you are!'

They laughed. It had been communication by phone for so long, and Mike had only ever seen Lida once in that brief meeting outside the embassy. 'For me that time you three girls were very much alike,' he explained.

'Oh, we remembered you all right,' Lida reassured him. 'You know,' she continued, 'there are some people you meet and talk to for a long time, yet you never really get to know them; but for others ten minutes is enough and you know you've found a friend.'

But Lida was exhausted. She had barely slept in those last three eventful days. A night on the overnight train from Chernogorsk had been followed by the long flight to Moscow from Krasnoyarsk. She had arrived late in the evening; a short night filled with anticipation, hopes and fears, her last night ever on Soviet soil, had been followed by a rushed morning. Then she had flown by herself out into the unknown, an exile for ever from her native land where she had experienced the guiding hand of God amidst the dramas and depths of her thirty years of life.

So Mike and Danny mounted guard over Lida, refusing to let anyone speak to her until she had caught up with some sleep. Later she told them she had spent hours just standing under the shower, almost as if she were letting her old life be washed away. And then she slept, ready to face the reporters, phone calls and scores of unknown friends and well-wishers, together with 'the whole circus of people', as Mike put it, who turned up the next day.

In the midst of everything Mike and Lida managed to snatch time just to sit and talk and fill in some of the gaps in the story.

'How terrible we felt that day we went into the embassy,' she recalled. 'We didn't know whom we could trust. All we knew was that if they forced us back on to the street it would be the end.'

Five years exactly from that eventful day in 1978 all the rest of the Vashchenko family flew together to Vienna, where Lida was allowed to go right out on to the tarmac to meet them. In the interim Lida had gone on to Israel, and two days after she arrived there, her parents and sisters made the momentous decision to leave the American Embassy and go home to Chernogorsk too, trusting that it would work out for them as it had done for Lida. Mike, who was in touch with the family by phone, was able to relay this piece of news to Lida, who could only pray and wait for the final outcome.

But the saga was not quite over. The family flew on to Israel from Vienna. They spent a month there, but when they applied for permanent residence they experienced a major setback. They did not fit into Israel's immigration laws. After the initial shock, however, they found that a travel agency had a group cancellation that very same day and could fly the entire family on to the USA.

They are now living in Seattle and Idaho. Lida is in St Louis where she is working for the United Pentecostal Church, trying to win publicity for the cause of Christians and Jews who wish to emigrate from the USSR. The other family involved in the drama, the Chmykhalovs, received their visas to emigrate three weeks after the Vashchenkos and they are now in the USA as well.

It is a happy conclusion and Keston's role in the story was substantial. The College provided essential background information from its archives for the Churches and the campaign who supported the Siberian Seven, as well as an advisory service. Mike maintained a rewarding, though often strenuous, personal link which was of immense value to the family who often felt that officialdom largely ignored them. Mike's quiet faith harmonized with theirs. In him the family found a friend and a focus. The phone calls he made to Lida, and to Lyuba and the others in Moscow, in the agonizing months of uncertainty, were vital to them and to the work of Keston as it tried to keep alive the interest which the family had aroused by constantly supplying the media with information.

This work is done by the Information Department which produces a fortnightly information bulletin, the *Keston News Service*, as well as instant bulletins by telex. The department is run by Alyona Kojevnikov with Sandra Oestreich as her assistant, both deeply committed to the work they do. Alyona was born in Yugoslavia in a Russian family, lived in displaced persons' camps and was brought up in Australia, but is unmistakably Russian in her whole outlook. Her work at Keston enables her to focus her interest on the homeland she has never lived in, but has integrated into her personality. Sandy too has travelled widely. 'The quiet call of God' which came to her when she was a student has taken her far beyond her family's Wisconsin farm to Sweden and then to Yugoslavia where she worked as a missionary among students in Zagreb. Her family found it hard to take at first, but Sandy simply obeyed an inner voice and went where it seemed to be leading.

She spent three and a half years in Zagreb, but found it tough going as a single woman. Christian friends counselled her about considering other areas of work in Eastern Europe. She had heard Michael Bourdeaux speak in Sweden about his work and so she applied to Keston College, where she has fitted in, doing whatever needs to be done.

'If you're at Keston and there's a job to be done you just

go ahead and do it!' she declares. 'Of course some people have specific gifts, and they get used to the full. Alyona, for instance, is the best interpreter I've ever heard. She captures the spirit of the speaker as well as the literal meaning of the words.'

Keston has benefited from Sandy's adaptability, but she in her turn has gained depths and insights. 'The work done here has made me aware of the riches of spirituality in the Catholic and Orthodox churches,' she says. 'Working at Keston has helped me deepen my own evangelical convictions, while at the same time it's made me less intolerant of others. People are always afraid that tolerance will weaken your own convictions, but it's had quite the opposite effect for me. It's narrowed me down to basic Christian convictions and at the same time it's enlarged me. There's a difference between depth of conviction and narrowness, and that's something important I've learnt since coming here.'

Orthodox spirituality has made considerable impact on other people at Keston too. Michael has written about what it has meant to him in *Risen Indeed*, where he has highlighted some of the riches of a tradition too little understood by Christians in the West. Philip Walters, the Research Director of Keston College, has also found that his study of Orthodoxy and the time he has spent in the Soviet Union with Orthodox Christians have enlarged his own horizons. As a postgraduate in Moscow he was able to talk to young Christians with minds as eager as his own about the ideas of religious thinkers from Russia's past whose writings are not available in the Soviet Union except to a handful of privileged specialists. His access to libraries which were denied to the young Russians who were to become his friends forged a link between the Cambridge graduate and his contemporaries in Moscow. It was a heady time, a time of religious awakening when it was suddenly conceivable to 'want the whole world', as Vladimir Poresh declared.

Yet there was a heavy price to pay. Some of Philip's Russian friends are in labour camp now, not yet middle-aged, but the ripples left by the plunge they took from scientific materialism into faith are spreading still, despite appalling repression. Their Christian witness left its impact on

Philip too. He finds his work at Keston a way of channelling his academic interests into areas which will enable a vision glimpsed in tiny flats in Moscow to become reality. If the world wakes up and listens and understands, the right to believe can yet be won.

[1] *Keston News Service*, no. 2, 19 June 1974.
[2] *KNS*, no. 31, 28 October 1976.

8

'Rainbow-coloured hopes'

As it enters the Church the Russian intelligentsia is flowing into the main channel of Russia's great culture: the prodigal son is returning to his Father and discovering in our Lord Jesus Christ the solution to all his problems.

Tatyana Goricheva.[1]

Christ was revealed to us in no speculative manner: we met him, we saw him moving across our land. This encounter was a turning point in our life.

Feliks Svetov.[2]

In the early seventies the documents published in the innovatory journal *Religion in Communist Lands*, which was edited by Xenia Howard-Johnston and existed even before Keston College moved into its permanent premises, devoted considerable attention to the struggles of evangelical Christians—leaders like Georgi Vins and Josif Ton, as well as to the sufferings of families. There were many heart-rending appeals from mothers whose children had been taken from them, daughters who had seen their fathers arrested, wives left alone to bring up their families with no source of support.

The Orthodox Church is represented too, but at first mainly in the form of spiritual writings, sermons and prayers, which had often not been published anywhere else and which show how impoverished our own Western culture often is for all its gloss and attractiveness.

The cross of Christ is the banner of a Christian. The unavoidable bearing of life's cross, completed under the shadow of the Lord's Cross, is lightened and sweetened by the power of God and becomes a ladder, raising the Christian from earth to heaven.[3]

Our relative affluence tends to make Westerners afraid of suffering, so that when grief, long-term illness, bereavement, handicap, death hit us or our families we no longer know how to cope. Affliction makes us social pariahs, lepers, outcasts, even slaves, as Simone Weil has pointed out in *Waiting on God*. As a society we tend to be kinder to our pets than to the grossly handicapped among us. The Letters of Spiritual Counsel from a martyred Orthodox bishop written during prison and exile in the thirties[4] provide a deeper insight into life than our coffee-table, pre-packaged culture usually offers.

No one can live through life without his Gethsemane or his Golgotha . . .

Sometimes in impatience you say . . . 'Why did you send me this cross?' And the cross answers with your lips: 'It was sent to me for this: to show me my shortcomings, so that I might understand what is concealed in me. I thought I loved God and my neighbour, but now I see that there is no such love in me.'

We are always despondent and sad that we do not have a calm and sorrowless life. I don't know about you, but I always think that such peace is the same as everyday security: a small flat, firewood, food and so on. The Fathers say of this peace that it is the chief and most perfidious enemy . . .

You grieve because your life has been and continues to be not as you would have wanted it . . . But we must, even at the eleventh hour of our life on earth, learn to live according to the wise proverb of the people: 'Live not as you want, but as God commands.' Don't wish, says Avva Dorofei, that everything should happen as you want, but wish that it be as it is (that is, as God arranges) and thus you will be at peace with all.

To explain to God 'you must save me like this and like that' is impossible because salvation as a gift of God is above human comprehension. God leads man to his spiritual goals by paths which from outside have an unpleasant and unhappy character.

It is exactly this way of thinking which enables a young Orthodox believer living in Chernenko's Moscow to say sincerely, 'Prison was the best experience of my life; no, seriously. It deepened my faith and it taught me to pray.'

As early as 1973 *Religion in Communist Lands* records the religious awakening, the turning to Orthodoxy, the 'torrents of spring' which affected eager young minds. Their discoveries, their trials and their breaking fill the pages of later volumes of *RCL* as Orthodox believers find the same reckless faith as Aida Skripnikova and Georgi Vins. Boldly they proclaim truths they have discovered, enter the arena to fight for human rights, and, equally fearlessly, enter the other arena known by Christians since the earliest days of the Church: of captivity and suffering, a living martyrdom. Their bodies may not be gored by bulls or bear the toothmarks of leopards and lions, but they are cruelly marked all the same, starved, beaten and ill.

But why did Christian renewal awaken atheistic youth? After all, as believers themselves admit, the Church was enfeebled and restricted, virtually silenced and its liturgy phrased in an archaic language.

Quite simply, the time was ripe, as the wise old Christian dissident and champion of justice Anatoli Levitin remarked. Young people were tired of being given always the one and only ideology which no longer answered their questions or met their needs. Many turned, and still turn, as Valeri Barinov the rock musician notes, to drink and drugs, but some turn to Christianity.

Levitin is always highly readable and his article 'Religion and Soviet Youth'[5] analyses the religious revival among young people.

> The milieu of the young Soviet intelligentsia is most receptive to religion. You can sense religious ideas in the air when you are with these youngsters, so that sometimes only the gentlest of nudges is needed to bring someone to faith.

Less educated young people tend to be more attracted to Evangelical Christianity, notes Levitin, himself an Orthodox believer, who explains:

An Orthodox church service is incomprehensible to them with its unfamiliar language, rituals, strange clothes, and wailing old women. After five or ten minutes such a person shrugs his shoulders and leaves. Then he meets a simple fellow like himself who gives him a book containing the following words on the title page: 'The Holy Gospel of Our Lord Jesus Christ'. He starts reading; much of it is beyond him, much surprises him; but then he begins to read the Sermon on the Mount. Simple, clear words, something concerned with living today. He is soon introduced to evangelical Christians and meets people as simple as himself but people who do not drink alcohol, do not smoke, who reject debauchery and foul language. This is so unlike everything that surrounds him that these people seem to have come from another planet.

Levitin points out that the unselfish lives of simple, industrious, caring people is a great attraction, and indeed in prison camp (as Michael Bourdeaux has noted in *Risen Indeed*) such Christians make an immense impact on unbelievers and criminals. Levitin highlights the mutual goodwill and help which believers show one another, another great attraction, he says.

Vividly as ever, Levitin concludes:

All this indicates that Russian youth, awakening from its long sleep, is searching, that it has set out upon a journey. As a child I loved to walk to the early Liturgy in the winter. The Petersburg winter was cold and dark. Life had not yet awoken. The rare person in the street would be hurrying to work; he would slip, get up and start off again. And there, in the distance, would be the church which had only just been opened. The church would still be empty; only the odd pilgrim would be there, placing candles before the icons. One could feel the silence and expectation everywhere. I often feel that Russia is going through such a time of expectation now. The night is over. The sleepers are waking up. Life is beginning to stir. What will day be like?

Day was bright, rainbow-coloured indeed, but short-lived.

In a letter to Dr Philip Potter, General Secretary of the World Council of Churches, Alexander Ogorodnikov, driven to write out of concern for his friend who had been forcibly detained in psychiatric hospital, describes his own awakening and the subsequent harsh treatment he and his friends received:

> I am twenty-six years old. Three years ago I turned to God and became an Orthodox Christian. My friends made their way along the same path to the Church. Dissatisfied with the mere 'performance of a religious cult', having no opportunity to receive a religious education, and in need of brotherly Christian relations, we began in October 1974 to hold a religious and philosophical seminar, where we discussed such subjects as: The Church and the modern industrial world; A. Bergson's book *The Two Sources of Morality and Religion*; Vladimir Solovyov's concept of the God-Man; the sermons of Billy Graham, and so on.
>
> My friends and I grew up in atheist families. Each of us has followed a complex, sometimes agonizing path of spiritual questioning. From Marxist convictions, via nihilism and the complete rejection of any ideology, via attraction to the 'hippy' life-style, we have come to the Church.[6]

Alexander, or Sasha as his friends call him, was expelled from the State Institute of Cinematography in 1973 (he had planned to make a film about the 'Jesus People'). He was forced to move from one address to another because of constant close surveillance. He was dismissed from one job after another, all of them menial and far below his actual capabilities. He was insulted and mocked by the police and vilified in the press:

> What can I say about Ogorodnikov . . . he is morally a completely dissolute person. He doesn't work anywhere and leads, I would say, a parasitical way of life. Speaking bluntly, he is a swine . . .[7]

The seminar formed by Ogorodnikov and his friends in Moscow attracted some of the best and liveliest minds, mostly but not all young. They met in an atmosphere of trust, freedom and honesty; indeed truth was both paramount and heady. There was no self-seeking. Finding the official Church so closely controlled by the authorities that it could not begin to apply Christian ideas to the needs of the world at large, they met to talk and discuss freely, an intoxicating experience for minds kept in blinkers for so long. They found themselves bound together in community, in 'unity of the spirit in the bond of peace' or, as one member of the seminar most revealingly puts it:

It is not in isolated self-assertion, even if this involves creative activity, that we find the depths of our personality, but in fraternal love in the image of the Holy Trinity.[8]

They read avidly any Western religious literature they could get hold of, as Ogorodnikov outlines in his letter to Dr Potter. Above all, they read the Bible and the Early Fathers, as well as classic writers and the novelists and thinkers of the nineteenth century, in an effort to give themselves the sort of theological and philosophical education they could acquire nowhere else. They were fervent, sincere and fearless.

Young forces came out from the underground, eager for action. Everyone felt that we were standing on the brink of a new era, a new historical age.

There was one very important existential achievement: we conquered fear. We conquered it firstly on the level of everyday existence. We stopped being afraid that we would be sacked from our jobs, put in prison, sent into exile: it was all one to us. Secondly we conquered fear on the level of our inner life. We managed to conquer our neurotic inner fears by ceasing to live a life of denial and by becoming aware that what we had been afraid of until then was completely insubstantial. The myth that the KGB was all-powerful was exploded, the world was de-mystified: we saw ourselves no longer as victims but as creators.[9]

Thus Tatyana Goricheva sums up the beginnings of the movement. She was born in 1947, studied at Leningrad University, taught aesthetics, but then, coming under the surveillance of the KGB, was dismissed and worked at a variety of jobs, including that of a firewoman, until finally she was forced to break up her marriage and emigrate to the West.

Tatyana Goricheva was right. They *were* fearless, but one of the people who made a huge impact on them was a priest who was 'afraid all the time', yet spoke compellingly to hushed crowds in packed churches, relating basic Christian truths to everyday problems, even (as we saw in Chapter 5) to the problem of a believing child wearing a Pioneer's tie.

Young people crowded to hear Father Dmitri Dudko and spent hours in his cramped flat, talking till late at night, drinking tea and enjoying warm if meagre hospitality, even though Mrs Dudko looked askance at the long-haired 'weirdoes' in threadbare blue jeans. Older members of the congregation eyed them with some suspicion too.

'What are all these young people doing, coming here? They're not real believers. They've only come to listen to Father Dmitri,' complained one old lady.

'It doesn't matter that they don't believe yet,' her equally elderly friend replied, staunchly. 'They'll come to the faith in time. Just look what fine educated young people they are!'

But the same eye-witness who noted the conversation of the two old ladies also repeated:

> Once, after he had seen him on a previous occasion, a friend of mine had said, 'Why does he do it? I can't understand how he continues. He is quite different from Solzhenitsyn. I have spoken to them both. Solzhenitsyn simply was afraid of nothing and nobody, but this man is afraid all the time. Yet he carries on.[10]

He carried on and the authorities in the end played not on his fear, but on his humility, convincing him that his unique sermons were nothing but a huge ego-trip, a colossal piece of arrogance, aimed at downing his superiors in the Moscow patriarchate. After five months' imprisonment he was made to appear on television and admit his guilt publicly. Father Dmitri, no stranger to prison and labour camp, did so smiling, which made his friends fear that euphoria-inducing drugs might have been used.

Thus they silenced him. He still works as a priest, and he is not the only person to have been broken. One Pentecostal believer recalls how her pastor, having been tortured, called at her family's home. Overjoyed at hearing the familiar voice, and thinking that the pastor had been released from prison, the girl's father hurried to open the door, and was pounced on by KGB men, who used the erstwhile pastor to arrest many believers that dreadful night.

Everything in the room was turned inside out; they felt in every corner of the mattresses, pillows, the patched blankets, our clothes. Only the earth floor was not dug up. We sobbed. 'Please let me pray with my wife and children for the last time.' 'Go on then, pray, perhaps your God will help you,' the policemen said sarcastically. We all fell on our knees, wept and sobbed, feeling the presence of the Spirit. 'That's enough, stop now,' the policeman broke in anxiously. 'We haven't much time.'[11]

What is it like to be harassed, watched and followed? Alexander Ogorodnikov in his letter to Dr Potter speaks only sketchily about his own experience when the KGB began to hound him. 'After this they really began to hunt me. My flat, of which I had been deprived together with my work, was surrounded by a militia detail which tried to break down the door. I could not even fetch my books and belongings.'

He describes the sufferings of his friends in more detail. A seriously ill elderly woman, the mother of a seminar member, was accosted by security men as she lay in bed and questioned as to her son's movements, while a 21-year-old girl who attended the seminar was treated like this by two men in civilian clothing:

In the street, in the metro and on the trolleybus they surrounded her closely, shoved her, trod on her feet and shouted, 'Why are you treading on people's feet!' When she went out of the metro one of them hit her abruptly and unexpectedly on the back, then in the street he hit her again. They went with her, breathing down her neck to her flat, and tried to break in after her!

Another seminar participant, continues Ogorodnikov, was beaten by three people 'using professional methods' who broke his arm and kicked him.

Two further seminar members, Alexander Argentov and Georgi Fedotov, were both interned in psychiatric hospital and their friends showed great concern for them, with Alexander Ogorodnikov and one or two others visiting them. Ogorodnikov himself was beaten up while serving a prison sentence of one year simply because he asked to see a priest. He was not released at the end of his sentence. Instead he was tried again on 30 September 1980 and was sentenced to six years in a strict regime camp, followed by five years' exile. At his trial Alexander said that this was his 102nd day on hunger strike as a protest against his trial. None of his family—even his wife—or his friends received permission to attend. His mother was allowed in, but was dismissed after ten minutes. 'Interested spectators from the general public' (in other words the KGB and hand-picked cronies) filled the court-room.

From a punishment cell in prison Alexander Ogorodnikov managed to write to his parents a letter which should fill anyone who cares for justice with concern. 'Rations are minimal, but I am refusing them,' he says and complains of lack of light, a 'refined torture', which causes his eyesight to deteriorate as he struggles to read the few books he is allowed in the semi-darkness of the cell.

> The administration is stepping up its efforts against me. I receive almost no letters, and the letters I write are either confiscated or not forwarded—that is why you do not hear from me. My dear forsaken ones, it would take a month to set down everything about my situation here, and it would be enough to fill a book. When I see you again, when I am out of prison, God willing, then I shall tell you all about it.[12]

If Alexander Ogorodnikov survives his eleven-year sentence (he will be released in 1991) he will be forty-one years old. He could have lived comfortably in Moscow with his attractive wife and their small son, making films, travelling, meeting friends. Instead he became a Christian. His horizons expanded to embrace ideas which are not permitted by the regime he lives under and now he endures a living death.

His friend Vladimir Poresh, another member of the seminar, was called as a witness at Alexander's trial and loyally tried to take all the blame himself. He too is in prison now, sentenced to eight years. In a moving article describing the new mood which prevailed among young people Poresh affirmed that redemption comes through suffering. He wrote:

> God has given us a voice. There is no way back. Giving up is betrayal.
>
> We were born in dead and god-forsaken times, we lived as Pioneers and members of the Komsomol, but we want to die Orthodox Christians.
>
> The godless and blasphemous world of socialist realism is running away like sand between the fingers, and its dead skeleton stands naked. By inner spiritual strength we are throwing off the fetters of a reality to which we have been shackled—the fetters of a fantastic myth which has been set up as truth by use of force. Right (pravda) and Truth (istina), the Crucifixion and the redemptive sufferings of Our Lord Jesus Christ have revealed to us what genuine life is. A genuine perception of life is a tragic perception. The tragic is the opposite of humdrum vulgarity, just as truth is the opposite of the lie. One must not run away from tragedy, but strive for it with all the strength of one's soul. One must open one's heart to meet suffering, thanking the Lord for every wound.
>
> We must act in such a way that our faith does not simply become contemplative, estranged from life, but becomes actively incarnate in our life. . . We have to make a concrete and substantial response.[13]

Young people in the West too, living in an ethos of instant entertainment which values success above all else, and treading a path trodden by no previous generation between the pitfalls of unemployment and nuclear destruction, need these sane and dignified words; but to the man who penned them the State made a response which was concrete, substantial— and cruel.

In an article he managed to get through to Keston Vladimir Poresh describes in vivid detail how he was followed in Moscow all one evening and the whole of the next morning by the secret police. At first he was almost paralysed by fear, but as the number of 'watch-dogs' increased and stayed threateningly on his tail, he reports:

> I had completely come to myself now. I realized that fate had thrown me into a duel with evil forces, and that if I allowed fear to possess my soul they would have triumphed. . . . They had realized that I had seen them, but they were not trying to detain me, so they could only have had one aim: to frighten me, to victimize me, to paralyse my will and to destroy my dignity through fear. From that moment I stopped being afraid; fear was replaced by a sense of steady spiritual exaltation.[14]

Vladimir Poresh, or Volodya as his friends call him, came to faith only after traumatic searchings which led him to the verge of suicide. His agonizing was shared with a sympathetic lecturer who herself struggled with identical problems and was coming towards the same amazing conclusions, in spite of the age gap between them of nineteen years and their vastly different experience of life. Tatyana Shchipkova, a highly qualified and much valued lecturer at Smolensk, taught 17-year-old Volodya French. He was, she recalls, 'a tall adolescent with large hands and honest, kind eyes, a simple person without the faintest suspicion of the existence of the camps and convinced that religion developed as the result of fear of the forces of nature'.

Volodya went on to Leningrad University and there, plunged in anxiety, he realized how senseless life is without spirituality. He wrote to Tatyana, describing his heart-searchings. Even the search for God seemed senseless, he thought, but he would keep on searching for that very reason.

'At last,' writes Tatyana,[15] 'after these meanderings, the crisis came in 1970: the total recognition of his own spiritual enslavement and that of everyone around him.'

He came to see Tatyana and was so changed she thought something terrible had happened. So upset was he indeed that he did a very un-Russian thing and sat down without taking off his heavy winter coat.

'I understand everything!' he declared.

'What do you mean?' Tatyana asked.

'Everything' Volodya repeated, and Tatyana nodded sympathetically. She understood, of course she understood! She too was searching. She too was moving towards faith, to the conclusion that God must exist or everything was senseless.

The marvel is that after fifty-three years of official atheism such a conversation took place at all, and that it found its way out to the West.

It took Volodya four years to grope his way to faith and the seminar was of immense significance to him. He was baptized on 20 October 1974. He was twenty-five years of age.

By then Tatyana Shchipkova was making the journey from Smolensk to Moscow to join in meetings of the seminar too. She had been born in 1930 and had lived through the siege of Leningrad in which her mother had died. Eleven-year-old Tatyana then went to live with her grandmother. She graduated in French and taught in Smolensk for seventeen years and was much loved by her students. In 1972 she was awarded a higher degree for a thesis in Romance languages, including Romanian, a highly praised work which won considerable academic acclaim.

So Tatyana had everything to lose in becoming a member of the seminar, but her conviction that what she was finding was true led her willy-nilly among young people twenty years her junior, whose discussions gave her something she had never found anywhere else, neither at academic conferences, nor over cups of tea with her highly respectable friends. In the draughty shack loaned by the clinic where Alexander Ogorodnikov worked as a caretaker Tatyana found the warmth of Christian contact and unhampered freedom of thought in the field of spirituality.

She became involved with the journal *Community* which was produced by the seminar, and on 21 May 1978 her flat was searched. Seven copies of the journal (one of which reported news of the arrests of Baptists) were confiscated. Tatyana was interviewed by the KGB and charged with anti-Soviet activity. Retribution was swift and automatic. A campaign was mounted to attack her professionally.

For years Tatyana had included in her first-year Latin classes lessons on the Roman world in the first century, which dealt with the beginnings of Christianity, with the person of Christ, his teachings and the part played by Christianity. It was a brave enough thing to do and the classes were popular and well attended. Now, knowing that the axe was about to fall, she explained that the Christian religion was still practised—the first time the students had ever been told this by a teacher—that it was attracting more and more educated people, in the Soviet Union as well as elsewhere, and that she herself had now become a believer.

> I explained what it meant to be a Christian and how I had become one. Towards the end of the class I warned the students that, although I had done nothing illegal or immoral, I was not sure whether I would be allowed to continue working with them. We are not in the habit of telling the truth about ourselves, and so the students were unaccustomed to hearing it. They were stunned by what I said, listened in total silence and did not ask a single question.[16]

A unanimous decision was taken by the department to dismiss Tatyana. 'Teachers simply do not have rights to a large number of things, for example certain sorts of clothes or hair-styles and even more so certain beliefs,' one colleague told her.

Tatyana was allowed to speak in her own defence and had an interesting comment to make about her audience's reaction.

> As far as I could judge, what they and the others had found most difficult was to take in the fact that the person standing before them actually held and acted on beliefs, whatever they might be. Some found it hard to accept that it was possible to do this kind of thing, and others rejected the right to do so.
>
> Some of those who spoke branded me as a hypocrite and liar. The latter accusation sounded strange, to say the least, considering that it came at the very moment that I had ceased lying.

Tatyana Shchipkova was dismissed from the institute for being insufficiently qualified for the job she had been doing, with excellent reports, for seventeen years. She was warned officially that if she continued to maintain contact with Christian groups she would face criminal charges for having intentionally circulated fabrications defaming the Soviet state and social order.

At forty-eight she was stripped of all her academic awards, her higher degree was rescinded and she was forced to start looking for another job. She was refused employment everywhere, while at the same time the local police harassed her for being unemployed.

On 10 October 1979 Tatyana Shchipkova was arrested and sentenced to three years in general regime camps. The authorities of Smolensk Institute who had once valued her as one of their best tutors described her as ignorant, vulgar and high-handed. During transportation to the camps she was very ill with a glaucoma but was refused any treatment. A year later when her son Alexander visited her he found his mother ill with dysentery and discovered that her eyesight was failing.

'The race is now on, and it is now only a question of what comes on first, death or blindness,' Tatyana said.[17]

She was released in January 1983 and in broken health at fifty-three years of age, her glaucoma untreated still, she is working as a cleaner. Her son Alexander has been threatened with arrest and will be brought to trial if he does not give up his religious activities. But Alexander, young as he is, has learnt to pray. He knows, as Vladimir Poresh wrote to him while he was doing his military service: 'Prayers are a great help to those going through an ordeal.'

The churches in the West tend to know this in theory. Christians in the Soviet Union, living with fear, harassment, arrest, torture and imprisonment, vilified and punished for their faith, know that prayer is the only thing which sustains them. They have found an inner freedom no force on earth can destroy, so that Anatoli Levitin, in his sixties, writes from a cramped prison cell, where he was incarcerated with criminals and interrogated daily: 'Not only my prayer, but much more the prayer of many faithful Christians helped me. I felt it continually, it worked from a distance, lifting me up as though on wings, giving me living water and the bread of life, peace of soul, rest and love.'[18]

The work of Keston College in keeping the world informed about the silenced churches of Eastern Europe is a vital aid to prayer. Faced repeatedly with closure of the College, because of lack of financial backing and support, Michael Bourdeaux has nevertheless seen his work grow. New openings have occurred as far away as China. If only there were the resources to develop them. In the Soviet Union the great longing for truth which exploded into Christian renewal remains unfulfilled, but, forced underground, continues to enrich the lives of people who have now become even more fearful.

For this reason it is vital that Keston should continue to fulfil Michael's vision and be a voice for those who are silenced as they endure injustice. Linked closely to the cause of human rights, however, is another factor which makes Keston's work essential: the deep inner workings of the spirit which is ultimately the only salvation for us all. And the persecuted churches in the Soviet Union are a vibrant wholesome force for the whole world. Dostoyevsky spoke with a prophetic voice when he wrote:

> In their solitude they keep the image of Christ pure and undefiled for the time being, in the purity of God's truth, which they received from the Fathers of old, the apostles and martyrs, and when the time comes they will reveal it to the wavering righteousness of the world. That is a great thought. That star will shine forth from the East.[19]

Dostoyevsky is thinking specifically of Russia's monks, but his words are true of Alexander Ogorodnikov, languishing in the near darkness of his cell, Vladimir Poresh in his prison, Tatyana Shchipkova on her knees in the damp, her hands in dirty water, ill and going blind. Their star is shining from the East, revealing to the 'wavering righteousness' of the West depths of spirituality with which we are, on the whole, unfamiliar.

This chapter began with spiritual writings gathered up by Keston College and published in its journals. Let it end with an extract from a meditation from the same source, for Michael's work has made a major contribution to our starved inner lives by making the riches and faith of Russian believers known and unknown available to us. That too is something which must continue.

Let misfortunes rain down on my head like water, let them drum and drum and drum, whispering: 'Curse, curse, curse Him, that is the only freedom you have.'—I will merely lower my head further and clench my teeth harder, I will not say anything to anyone and I will not hear anything from anyone. Tears of gratitude will stream from my eyes. I will not wipe them away and feel ashamed. I have nothing to be ashamed of. I will kiss Your hand, light the lamp, kneel down and whisper a prayer of gratitude, because I have realized that for me happiness lies only in misfortune. Why do You love me so, Lord, why do You trust me so? Not as a slave, but as a friend.

. . . I believe that when I have drunk the whole cup that You have given me, drunk it to the dregs, on the far side of suffering which *they* call madness, there will be a door, and I will go through the door, and there will be a blue sky and a warm blue sea. I shall swim and swim, barely moving the tips of my fingers, now in the blue sky, now in the warm sea. But it is not a sea, but a caress, a whole sea of caresses for me alone, a worm like me, and it is not a sky but grace, sheer, boundless grace without pebbles or thorns. Eternity for me alone. Others have their own eternities. In my Father's house there are many mansions. Glory to Thee, O Lord.

I will not hurry You. You Yourself know when; when I will be able to drain the cup. Your devoted slave. What a beautiful word.[20]

[1] 'The Religious Significance of Unofficial Soviet Culture', *Religion in Communist Lands*, vol. 8, no. 3, autumn 1980.

[2] 'An open letter in the case of Zoya Krakhmalnikova', *RCL*, vol. 11, no. 2, summer 1983.

[3] St Tikhon of Zadonsk writing in the eighteenth century, *RCL*, vol. 1, no. 1, January–February 1973.

[4] *RCL*, vol. 2, no. 1, January–February 1974

[5] *RCL*, vol. 7, no. 4, winter 1979.

⁶ *RCL*, vol. 4, no. 4, winter 1976.

⁷ Quoted in *RCL*, vol. 5, no. 3, autumn 1977.

⁸ Quoted in Philip Walters, 'The Ideas of the Christian Seminar', *RCL*, vol. 9, nos. 3–4, autumn 1981.

⁹ Tatyana Goricheva, 'The Religious Significance of Unofficial Soviet Culture', *RCL*, vol. 8, no. 3, autumn 1980.

¹⁰ *RCL*, vol. 4, no. 2, summer 1976.

¹¹ 'Pentecostal Dossier', *RCL*, vol. 5, no. 3, autumn 1977.

¹² Quoted in *Christian Prisoners in the USSR 1983–4*. Keston College 1983.

¹³ *RCL*, vol. 9, nos. 3–4, autumn 1981.

¹⁴ *RCL*, vol. 8, no. 2, summer 1980.

¹⁵ Ibid.

¹⁶ Ibid.

¹⁷ *Keston News Service*, no. 122, 24 April 1981.

¹⁸ RCL, vol 2, no. 2, March–April 1974; quoted by Michael Bourdeaux, *Risen Indeed*. Darton, Longman and Todd, 1983.

¹⁹ *The Brothers Karamazov*, vol. 1, trans. David Magarshack.

²⁰ 'Meditation', Moscow 1972. *RCL*, vol. 4, no. 3, autumn 1976.

9

'Help me to bear it'

Anyone who knows the risen Christ has a heavy responsibility placed upon himself. He must bring to people the news of Christ's resurrection, in whatever way he can and wherever destiny leads him. If you've been with Mary to Christ's tomb, if you've been convinced that it's empty because Christ is risen, then go and tell everyone about it. Christ is risen! May God bless you and help you.

Father Dmitri Dudko[1]

They want to drag a new cross on top of me—help me to bear it so that afterwards we can sing together.

Father Dmitri Dudko[2]

Women as well as men suffer in prison and in psychiatric hospital, as we have seen. And women have been in the forefront of the human rights movement. Crying 'help me to bear it', they have managed to get document after document out of the country, often at great personal risk, accurately describing the sufferings of their families. We have already seen how Aida attended trials of believers and was one of the first to risk arrest in order to 'tell the West' the true story of persecution. Large families were often left without means of support when husbands and fathers were dismissed from work and then put into prison. As long ago as the sixties a group of Baptist women organized themselves into the Council of Prisoners' Relatives; while in the seventies among the Orthodox women believers there has been a real attempt to relate Christian truths for the first time to women's issues.

Despite the fact that the Communist world holds an annual 'International Women's Day', women have a hard life in the Soviet Union and elsewhere in Eastern Europe. There are few labour-saving devices. Families work long hours and most city people face a journey home on overcrowded public transport out to the huge tower blocks which house the majority of the population. Then shopping has to be done, with inevitable queues, food has to be prepared, children are returned by Granny from play-school and the mother has to cope with her tired toddler. A particular hardship for women is the relatively low standard of the maternity hospitals; abortion is a common substitute for contraception.

It was in recognition of these hardships, together with a feeling of impatience at being treated always as inferior by her male colleagues (who praised her for her masculine mind!), that Tatyana Goricheva, who founded the religious seminar in Leningrad, helped to launch an unofficial journal called *Woman and Russia* in 1979. She was a target for intense KGB pressure and in 1980 was expelled from the Soviet Union, together with two other women involved in editing *Woman and Russia*. One of these was Yuliya Voznesenskaya, whose description of the plight of women prisoners has been quoted in Chapter 6.

The Baptist and Orthodox churches seldom, if ever, air women's questions. The leadership is exclusively male, although recently for the first time in its history the patriarchate has taken women into its training by paying the stipends of twenty women (a hundred actually applied) at the Leningrad School of Music who are studying with a view to participating in the singing of the liturgy. Trying to find a Christian model for themselves, the Orthodox women took Mary, the mother of the Lord, and have formed an independent religious group called the 'Mary Club' with its own journal. This whole movement has been viewed with very little sympathy, on the whole, by feminists in the West who find it difficult to appreciate the Russian women's Christian standpoint and their opposition to Marxism. Very low-key reporting of the group has reached the press in the United Kingdom, though there is more contact with women in West Germany where Tatyana Goricheva and Yuliya Voznesenskaya now live.

Yuliya describes the birth of the movement thus:

We came by different routes to the decision to speak and act in the name of the women of our country . . . We viewed Russia through a prism of religious revival. We did not thirst for a social and political revolution, but for the only important revolution—that of the spirit. We firmly decided that in our work we would not follow the pattern of western feminists, although much of their wide movement was close to our hearts . . . we decided to go our own way and develop a women's movement in Russia along Russian lines.[3]

Among the eight founder-members of the Mary Club was a young artist, Nataliya Lazareva. Nataliya was born in 1947 in Leningrad, but her mother's ill-health meant that from a very early age she had to spend lengthy periods in children's homes, where of course the upbringing was entirely atheistic. She was given no chance to develop her artistic talent; instead she was sent to work in a factory before she had completed her secondary schooling. By dint of great determination Nataliya finished a course at a 'school for young workers' and took a diploma thereafter, but found it impossible to get a job in Leningrad and was unable to look elsewhere for work because of her mother's ill-health. As an unemployed person she received no benefit. Then she managed to get a part-time job for a very small wage teaching in a children's artistic circle; but the group soon dissolved for lack of funds. Nataliya was forced to work as a stoker in a gas works. The only thing which made such heavy work bearable was the fact that she met two Christians there, a poet who had been involved with the Moscow seminar and a literary critic whose quest for faith had led him to the Leningrad group. In spite of heavy work and long hours Nataliya continued to give lessons free of charge to talented children who had belonged to the group. One of these was the son of Yuliya Voznesenskaya. A close friendship developed between the two women.

In spite of her atheistic upbringing Nataliya became a Christian and was baptized into the Orthodox Church. The Mary Club got off the ground in March 1980. There was instant police reaction. Most of the founders were expelled from the USSR; but, contrary to the expectations of the KGB, the movement did not die, though it was forced to go underground. Nataliya was arrested in September 1980.

At her trial three months later the judge demanded why, contrary to claims in the Soviet Press, Nataliya insisted that the life of women in the USSR is exceptionally hard. To this Nataliya answered, 'Because I cannot say that black is white.'

She was sentenced to ten months in a labour camp. The women were forced to do heavy work and suffered constant hunger. In these conditions of despair Nataliya gave her fellow-prisoners a good deal of support, sharing her meagre rations with them and writing letters and protests against unjust treatment on behalf of other women.

Nataliya Lazareva, whose spell in prison was marked by such truly selfless Christian behaviour, was rearrested less than a year after her return to Leningrad. She was accused of passing documents to foreigners, was charged with anti-Soviet activity and sentenced to four years' strict regime camp followed by two years in exile. 'No other regime is so afraid of its own women,' comments Yuliya Vosnesenskaya.[4]

The lot of a writer in her mid-fifties, Zoya Krakhmalnikova, was equally harsh. Zoya and her husband, Feliks Svetov, both lived quite comfortably in Moscow as members of the Soviet literary establishment until, as Feliks put it, '. . . we came to the Church, to God, to Christ.'[5]

Aware of the great dearth of Christian literature 'in an atmosphere where there was poverty, hunger and the absence of God's word', as her husband explains, Zoya Krakhmalnikova set to work to compile a journal called *Hope*, to which she also contributed articles. The journal had the private blessing of the hierarchy of the church and contained absolutely nothing political, aiming only to give religious sustenance with an emphasis on the value of spirituality and the power of prayer. Various numbers of *Hope* contained sermons, letters of spiritual help, testimonies and prayers, and contemporary Orthodox theology, as well as works of the Early Fathers not available anywhere else. Some copies reached the West, but as Zoya pointed out, once the journals had become public property she had no more control over them.

After searches carried out in her Moscow flat, her son's flat and the holiday house where she was staying with her daughter and baby grandson, Zoya was arrested at 4 one morning and sentenced on 1 April 1983 to a year in a strict regime camp and five years of exile. She is now serving this sentence, far away in the Altai region of the USSR which borders on Mongolia, a distance of more than 3000 kilometres from Moscow.

What does this sentence mean for a 55-year-old Christian woman, not in the best of health? Zoya is kept in the company of criminal prisoners. The transportation, as we have seen from Nijole's experience, is appalling and exile in remote places is fraught with danger. Absolutely anything can happen from being robbed, molested or physically assaulted to being faced with more criminal charges and rearrest simply on the whim of local authorities. And even when her period in exile is over Zoya will be refused permission to return to Moscow for another three years. She will be sixty-four years old before she is able to live with her family again.

Yet it must be stressed, all that Zoya has done has been to disseminate spiritual literature. And even when her husband and she produced articles in *samizdat* journals they did so openly, signing their own names, refusing any compromise or lie which 'is impossible when one is writing of Christ', as Feliks Svetov points out.

No wonder Michael, in a letter in spring 1984 to supporters of the work of Keston College, writes, 'Now more than ever is the time to challenge the new [Chernenko] leadership to grant real religious liberty.'

In January 1980 an impassioned statement signed by Zoya and Feliks arrived at Keston College. The appeal, dated November 1979, was on behalf of an outstanding priest, Father Gleb Yakunin, who played a key role in the human rights movement of the seventies. His arrest, wrote Zoya and Feliks, was a blow 'at the very heart of living, suffering Russia', for Father Gleb was known to everyone as a man who had no fear in speaking out strongly in defence of religious liberty.

Gleb Yakunin was born in Moscow on 4 March 1934. While studying forestry in Irkutsk he met Father Alexander Men, a notable Orthodox priest. Men's life, together with the works of Russian philosophers such as Berdyayev, led Gleb Yakunin to a profound faith in Christ so that he decided to train for the priesthood. Accordingly, when he finished his studies, by then newly married to a wife who has supported him through strains and hardships, Gleb returned to Moscow, working for a pittance as a psalm-reader in a Moscow church. Amazingly (for it is far from easy to become a priest in the USSR), Gleb Yakunin was ordained on 10 August 1962 when Khrushchev's anti-religious campaign was at its height. Three years later, together with another young man who has since left the priesthood for family reasons, Father Gleb wrote an Open Letter to the Moscow patriarchate, outlining the tremendous pressures under which members of the Church were forced to live, and appealing to the patriarch to be more resolute in standing up to State interference. A similar declaration was sent to the Politburo. It was an almost unheard of step, as brave in its way as Aida's lonely protest in Leningrad on New Year's Eve. Other clergy who had agreed to sign backed off at the last moment, so the document went forward with only the two signatures. As a result Father Gleb was banned from office. He remained a priest, but was no longer allowed to officiate and received no salary.

At first his family—his wife, mother-in-law and now a small daughter—were forced to live off the generosity of friends, but eventually Father Gleb managed to get a variety of jobs in different Moscow churches, working as a janitor, a watchman and a reader. For a time no more news reached the West about a man who, many agree, together with Father Dmitri Dudko, has restored lay-people's trust in their Church which has too often been forced into servility in return for a few concessions from officialdom.

Then in 1975 Father Gleb and a layman, Lev Regelson, sent out to the Fifth Assembly of the World Council of Churches in Nairobi a highly charged document, possibly the single most effective *samizdat* appeal ever to have come out of the USSR. In it the writers appealed to the World Council to stop ignoring the problems of persecution in the USSR and to respond to the needs of prisoners and those in psychiatric hospitals. This document resulted in a serious examination by the West of religious persecution which was publicly debated in Nairobi for the first time. It was followed up by a letter to Dr Philip Potter on 6 March 1976 which analysed the Soviet legislation on religion, pointing out its built-in discrimination against religious believers.

In 1976 Father Gleb, wrongly believing he now carried international Christian opinion with him, formed, with two other Orthodox Christians, the Christian Committee for the Defence of Believers' Rights in the USSR. Its declared aim was 'to help believers exercise the right of living in accordance with their convictions' by advising and assisting believers of all denominations and documenting violations of their rights. It was a notable ecumenical step which was greatly appreciated by hard-pressed believers of all denominations who appealed warmly on behalf of Father Gleb when his arrest in 1979 became known.

'Whenever you meet Gleb Yakunin you feel joy and admiration for this selfless man,' wrote a group of Pentecostals in an appeal with 300 signatures, while a group of young Orthodox believers wrote to 'anyone who hears us', but particularly to members of the Catholic Church:

> [Father Gleb] is a fervently believing Christian, a man deeply attached to the Church, an Orthodox Christian who is open to everything that is best in other confessions. Fr Gleb's work in the Christian Committee for the Defence of Believers' Rights is self-sacrificing service of his neighbours. Thousands of people have appealed to the Committee and they have all received help and support. Fr Gleb's activity is based on strict observance of the laws of State and Church and he has worked openly in the sight of all.[6]

Even after Father Gleb's arrest the work of the Committee continued, but as the eighties have developed there are, in the words of Philip Walters of Keston College:

. . . signs that believers are now aware that the most tangible results of this kind of open campaigning are simply going to be further repression and imprisonments. The emphasis among Christian activists seems to be shifting towards discreetly coordinated religious self-education at the level of the private group or family in a more long-term effort to build an alternative moral basis for society. The emphasis is on love, integrity, honesty and the life of true community—all theoretical ideas of Marxism which are negated every day in practice.[7]

Father Gleb's trial was attended only by a hand-picked audience of stalwart atheists. Several witnesses who intended to support Father Gleb were not in the end admitted to the court. One witness, a church warden who had been expected to vilify him in her testimony, surprised the court by speaking well of him, saying that Father Gleb was a true Christian whom she was proud to know.

In reply to his lengthy sentence of five years in strict regime camps followed by five years in exile Father Gleb said, 'I rejoice that the Lord has sent me this test. As a Christian I accept it gladly.' After his trial he was allowed a short meeting with his wife and 16-year-old daughter, their last for a very long time. His two younger children were not present. Father Gleb had a special message for a friend who had recanted before the trial. He pleaded with his wife and all their friends not to be too harsh on him.

On 16 September 1981 Father Gleb began a hunger strike in a protest against the refusal of the authorities to allow Bibles and Gospels in prison. During his hunger strike he was force-fed very hot liquids which have left him with stomach ulcers. He outlined his reasons for abstaining even from the wretched prison diet thus:

Millions of believers who are confined to camps and prisons in our country are condemned to spiritual starvation. This ban is particularly ruinous to those who are sentenced to lengthy terms of deprivation of liberty . . . I believe in the coming resurrection of Russia. May she, like Lazarus, hear the miraculous call of the Almighty—'come forth'. Yet at the moment, while the reality of Russia is Golgotha, multitudes of the Faithful stand in dire need of your fraternal aid in defence of their rights.

Anatoli Levitin summed up the situation in his usual pithy way in an appeal to the Soviet authorities: 'Why are you so afraid? Do you think that the whole power of the Soviet Union will collapse if a priest reads the Bible?'

Father Gleb's personal, daily Golgotha continues. Suffering from high blood pressure, thin, his hair and beard shaved, deprived of visits from his wife, he has still over five years of imprisonment and exile ahead of him. Yet for many believers of every denomination in the Soviet Union and in the West his name is synonymous with hope: that resurrection will come, that faith will finally triumph and freedom and justice will prevail. For Father Gleb, as for so many other Christian prisoners, the fact that in the West there is a College with a voice raised on his behalf, and Christians who pray for him to 'help him to bear it', is something very important indeed. It is vitally important that the whole delicate, fraught process of *détente*, as well as the issues of human rights, should be firmly founded on truth; and Father Gleb has borne unswerving witness to that truth. He must not be allowed to be forgotten now that he has been silenced.

Keston's journal, *Religion in Communist Lands*, which is edited by Jane Ellis, is still the only periodical in English which deals systematically with the whole question of believers under atheism. The plight of Jews, Buddhists, Muslims and other religious minorities in the USSR is discussed as well as that of Christians. And from its earliest days the journal has had a wider view than simply the countries in Eastern Europe. Articles have appeared on China (including one on Jews in China) and on Cuba, while early in 1984 there was an article on Nicaragua in order to keep readers 'informed about the present situation in a country where an avowedly Marxist government has recently come to power and where the Churches have had to work out their response to a new political situation'.[8]

It might be of interest, as this chapter closes, to scan the contents of 1984's first number of *Religion in Communist Lands*. As well as the article on Nicaragua, there are two on Hungary and one on 'Islam in the Afghan Resistance'. Poland is well represented with an article on the Pope's 1983 visit, a 'photo-story' of the funeral of a pro-Solidarity priest, and a fascinating document on the life of a Polish priest in Kazakhstan who, like Father Lizna, found himself serving prisoners and glimpsing from time to time kindness even among his persecutors. Arvan Gordon, another member of the Keston team, has an article on the Luther Quincentenary in the German Democratic Republic, reflecting the Church's independent stance under a totalitarian regime. Soviet press articles surveyed in the journal show that the pressures are as fierce as ever, believers are slandered as 'smart operators' and even 'werewolves', while Keston College is cited by the Soviet Press as being one of 'twenty-five organizations in Western Europe alone engaged in gathering religious intelligence about socialist countries—under the mask of false holiness'. The religious *samizdat* gives news of some of the people mentioned in this book, including letters from Valeri Barinov, the rock musician, and his friend Sergei Timokhin, who appeal 'to world public opinion to defend them and their families, and for prayer'. News of Anatoli Shcharansky, who experienced the happiness of Hanukah in his cell, is grave indeed. His mother's appeal for him to be released early on health grounds was turned down, even though Andropov on 21 January 1983 had stated to the General Secretary of the French Communist Party that convicts like Shcharansky could be released before their full sentence is completed.

Jane Ellis, the editor, is also deeply concerned for Father Gleb Yakunin and other Orthodox believers. She has been drawn gradually to a deep awareness of the Orthodox Church and has herself established an organization to help them practically, Aid to Russian Christians (ARC). This chapter began with women in Russia. Perhaps the next chapter should start with one English Christian woman's concern for the Orthodox Church and take up Jane's story from the day when a group of students met together to pray.

[1] *Our Hope*. St Vladimir's Seminary Press, 1977.

[2] Sermon on Sunday 1 October 1972; *Religion in Communist Lands*, vol. 1, nos. 3–4, autumn 1973.

[3] 'The Independent Women's Movement in Russia', *RCL*, vol. 10, no. 3, winter 1982.

[4] *RCL*, vol. 10, no. 3, winter 1982.

[5] *RCL*, vol. 11, no. 2, summer 1983.

[6] *RCL*, vol. 8, no. 4, winter 1980.

[7] 'Christians in Eastern Europe: a Decade of Aspirations and Frustrations', *RCL*, vol. 11, no. 1, spring 1983.

[8] *RCL*, Editorial, vol. 12, no. 1, spring 1984.

10

'A far land opens wide before me'

When the rowanberry reddens,
Clustered moist in autumn leaves,
When the executioner silently
Drives through my hands the final nails
Then, through the blur of tears
With which I greet approaching death
A far land opens wide before me,
And on the river Christ toward me sails.
In his hands my hopes and dreams.
He wears my tattered clothes,
And on his hands, as rowanberries red,
He bears the pitiful marks of nails.
Christ, my country stretches out in sadness,
Upon this cross I am growing tired.
Will your small boat come and moor beside me
Where on high I languish, crucified.

Quoted by Anatoli Levitin[1]

Sometimes it happens in our lives that a single moment holds
such deep significance that it seems indeed as if 'a far land
opens wide' before our eyes. We may not even be aware
what this land really is, but the moment comes as a
turning-point. Such a moment came, we have seen, to Michael
Bourdeaux in a Moscow room, and the unknown land which
opened up for Michael as he responded to that quiet invi-
tation has been charted in the pages of this book. It is the
Keston story, and a team of people have their part in it. For
some of them, too, there was a moment which became very
significant, so that, looking back, they could say: 'This is
what led me here.' For others the moment, the meeting, the
encounter, whatever it might have been, opened up a whole

sequence of events which led them eventually to contact Michael and ask to share his work.

For Jane Ellis, a research worker and the editor of *Religion in Communist Lands*, this time came at prayer meetings with other students.

Jane first heard about the work of Keston College when she was still at school. A teacher told the Christian Union about the sufferings of Soviet believers, and Jane began to feel involved even then. When she started university, where she studied Russian, she quickly joined a prayer group which was set up to pray specifically for Christians in Communist countries. However, once the group got down to prayer they found it hard because they had really very little information. Jane contacted several Christian organizations asking for such information. She also wrote to Michael Bourdeaux, and so a contact began which was to lead Jane eventually to work with Keston College and also, at Michael's suggestion, to set up single-handed an organization called 'Aid to Russian Christians' which tries to provide what help it can to believers in need, though new laws and regulations have made that work very difficult. Jane studied in the USSR and, like her colleague at Keston, Philip Walters, found a ready kinship with young Orthodox Christians. From an evangelical background herself, she had until then very little understanding of the Orthodox Church, but the life and witness of the Christians she met, who were prepared to sacrifice their careers and their freedom for their faith, made such a deep impression on her that she has made a special study of Orthodoxy, and over the last months has been completing a book on it. Like Grazyna Sikorska from Poland, Jane finds that her work at Keston enables her to be true to her most deeply held beliefs.[2] 'The picture gets blacker and blacker,' she notes sadly, 'and yet, in spite of it all, there is growth.'

As long as the quiet persistent influence of Christians, praying and working for the truth, continues there is cause for hope. The great rivers of Russia freeze in the winter, but even so a small trickle sometimes breaks free, and where water flows ice eventually melts. The exhilarating spring days of the seventies, the 'torrents of spring' which awoke slumbering young minds, will come again; there is growth, after all; there is hope. The great longing of Christians including artists, thinkers and the young, even in Chernenko's Moscow, is to be allowed to find ways 'of expressing faith, true spirituality and religious belief'.[3]

The same growth and hope can be seen even as far away as China, where for so long there was even reason to fear that the Church and Christian belief had died.

The person who keeps Keston College informed about the research being done by experts on China is Arvan Gordon. Arvan came to the College in 1980 but his concern for the Church under totalitarian regimes began very many years earlier, on the eve of World War II, in fact. Arvan, then a student, watched a military parade in Berlin. He saw crowds salute the swastika, the broken cross which became the symbol of an evil regime, and wondered how Church people, who were undoubtedly among the crowd, could lift their right hands to salute something which stood as a complete denial of the teachings of Christ. He also heard of the death of a Protestant pastor in Buchenwald concentration camp.

Arvan went back to Germany in 1945 to the newly liberated concentration camp of Bergen-Belsen. There he saw at first hand the awful results of an ideology which had put its leaders and their politics above the welfare of its people. Once again Arvan wondered how the Church could have stood by and let it happen, but he was soon to hear more stories of the resistance of the Protestant 'Confessing Church' and of Roman Catholics who had chosen to die rather than support Hitler's regime. At the same time, a brief visit to the Soviet zone showed him clearly that in East Germany the Church had still to contend with a totalitarian government.

Study followed for Arvan. A degree at Cambridge in German and Dutch, and a diploma in theology linked his language interests with his faith. He taught and travelled, began to study Mandarin Chinese and, as Keston's work developed, took a keen interest in it, finally joining the team as a specialist on the German Democratic Republic. He also maintains a valuable link with research work on China, which could be developed even more were there the resources available to do so.

114

The Church in the GDR occupies a position which many more restricted Churches in the Warsaw Pact countries might envy, but this gives room for a more subtle temptation to dilute the specific demands of the Christian gospel merely to social welfare, important though that is in the Church's calling. Indeed, the Church undertakes a wide variety of welfare work and the authorities encourage such humanitarian service in this, the only Protestant Marxist State. (Catholics number something over a million, with nominal Protestants reaching something like eight million.) One problem facing the Churches in the GDR is how to bring a Christian voice to bear on the important issue of education: young people are strongly pressured to take an oath dedicating themselves to 'Socialism'. Another major issue is that of peace, for medium-range strategic nuclear weapons are being deployed in the GDR for the first time.

Religion in Communist Lands has published useful articles about the problems facing believers in the GDR, as well as elsewhere in Europe, and, as we have seen, in parts of Asia, China and Latin America. But Keston also produces a news-sheet called *The Right to Believe*, a title which aptly sums up Keston's aims and work. The Support Groups in Australia have taken up the idea and now publish their own *Right to Believe*, based on Keston's material. Readers of *RTB* have sent in warm, positive comments, showing that Keston's venture into newsprint has been much appreciated. *RTB* contains news of individual believers, and highlights some of the main developments in the countries researched by Keston College, noting their effect on Christians and others who are ready to sacrifice their freedom for the 'right to believe'.

In addition to the publications available from Keston ·which are mentioned in the notes of this book, the College has a sizeable library which stocks about 3000 volumes. The initial nucleus of these was donated by Michael; more than half are about the Soviet Union in all its aspects. Since 1980 the Polish section has expanded rapidly with more than 300 volumes in various languages. Any book-lover with an interest in Eastern Europe will find a treasure trove here. It is hoped that short study-courses may eventually be set up which would increase the importance of the library for readers outside the Keston College staff, who obviously make great use of the books in the course of their daily work. The College spends about £1,000 each year on books and is always grateful for donations.

The archive at Keston is a unique collection in the world. It has grown from small beginnings—Michael's collection of appeals from Soviet believers and press cuttings from Russian newspapers in the 1960s. After the move to Keston College, a remarkable character devoted a labour of love to classifying it: Mrs Shura Kolarz, a Russian *émigrée* who had long lived in London. Her husband had written an epoch-making book, *Religion in the Soviet Union*, published in 1961. He died very shortly afterwards but she invited Michael to meet her, nevertheless, and thus began a lifelong friendship. Offering her archivist training to Keston for nothing, Shura came weekly across London for years, until she was satisfied that the collection was correctly classified and housed.

Malcolm Walker, the present librarian and archivist, was born in Dunfermline but grew up in Manchester. His interest in the condition of believers in the Soviet Union was aroused by a visit there as part of his Russian studies. After graduating from the University of Bath, Malcolm worked at the University of Birmingham as a cataloguer of Russian books. He heard Michael speak at a meeting at the Selly Oak Colleges and realized then that there was a need for a librarian at Keston. A convinced Christian and a member of the Baptist church, Malcolm felt drawn to Keston's work which involves such large numbers of his fellow-believers in Eastern Europe and the USSR. He felt a deep respect for Michael's endeavours in the field of religious liberty and knew that he should like to play a part in that work himself.

And it is a continuing work. 'At the dawn of the Revolution,' notes Eduard Kuznetsov, a Jewish dissident, in his diaries, 'they sang gaily, "We'll destroy the churches and the prisons." They managed the first quite well, but there's been something of hitch with the second.'[4]

Until religious liberty is a reality in every country of the world Keston's work must go on. Meantime new facts, documents, letters, prayers and appeals flow in. Our story began with one girl, Aida of Leningrad. It is fitting that it should end with her counterpart, Galina Vilchinskaya.

Twenty-four-year-old Galina's faith is as fervent as Aida's and her testimony, even when she was falsely charged and rearrested after only three months of freedom following a three-year sentence, is as free from bitterness and as full of faith as Nijole Sadunaite's.

Galina was first arrested in 1979 while she was travelling home with a much persecuted pastor, Pavel Rytikov, and his son Vladimir, from a holiday camp for the children of Baptist prisoners. The children were scattered. All their belongings were confiscated, including 1600 roubles which had been set aside for fares and food. Galina was sentenced to three years in an ordinary regime camp. She was twenty-one years old, a member of an unregistered Baptist congregation in Brest which the authorities are currently hounding. Galina's father was told that if he got the church registered officially, Galina would be set free from prison. He refused, and Galina served her sentence. On her return, after spending a month with friends to try to build up her strength, Galina was invited to the Pacific coast to visit believers in Vladivostok. Her whole trip was monitored and on her return drugs were planted in her luggage. She was rearrested, held in prison and tried in February 1982.

The months preceding her trial were desperately hard for Galina. It was terrible to be wrongly accused and be put back into prison after such a short time of freedom. She shed many hopeless tears, which, however, she refused to let anyone see. Instead she spent a lot of time praying, even though there were four other women in her cell. 'At first they laughed and mocked,' she wrote, 'but now the room involuntarily goes quiet when I pray.' She was hungry too, but shared what food parcels her family were able to send with other prisoners. 'Pray for me,' she begged her family, 'It's all I ask. It's the only thing which helps me. God give me strength! I'm not the first one to suffer like this. I only want to go to the Father—forgive me, my tears are flowing . . . .'

But, even so, Galina could write that God had quietened her heart and given her strength. 'All this is in order to subdue my pride,' she wrote in a poem to her mother. 'It is to test my faithfulness, and see if my life really matches up to the things I profess. It isn't some unlucky stroke of chance. Our lives are in God's holy hands. He gives me a broad meadow and teaches me to live and work and not to grumble. The Lord will help me to carry the cross this time too. I want to be like him. I will not leave the way of Golgotha.'

The way out would have been quite easy. All she had to do was to agree to join a registered congregation. Her whole case is a deliberate attempt on the part of the authorities to undermine the cause of adherents of the unregistered churches (over whom the State has no other control) and to persecute members of the Council of Prisoners' Relatives, the Baptist human-rights group to which Galina's mother belongs. The elders of the registered church in Galina's home town of Brest (in the west of the USSR, next to the Polish border) were summoned the very day after her arrest in Vladivostok (as far away as it is possible to travel in the USSR, with a time difference of seven hours between the two places). The elders were informed that Galina had been found in possession of drugs and valuable sables and furs. This was clearly an attempt to discredit members of the unregistered church in the eyes of their fellow-believers.

Galina's behaviour in prison had been so exemplary that her defence lawyer actually did something almost unprecedented: she tried to get her acquitted! 'Medical evidence proves clearly that Vilchinskaya never used drugs and does not suffer from drug addiction. She is a disciplined worker who actually over-fulfils the usual work norms. She has a most positive character. I ask the court to deal justly with her and set her free.'

But the court refused to set Galina free, and refused too to take any fingerprints which might establish that the prints on the boxes of drugs found at the top of her bags were not hers. 'Science hasn't reached that far,' she was told repeatedly.

To Galina's joy her friends and family had made the long journey from home and were present in the court at her trial, a transcript of which has reached the West.

'I stand here only because I am a Christian,' Galina said,

and to her friends she added, 'Thank you that you've supported me and preserved me with your prayers.'

Galina's mother (who has been threatened with arrest for her work with the Council of Prisoners' Relatives) managed to dodge the guard and press flowers on her. 'Here you are, Galyochka,' she said. 'You've remained faithful and not trodden the path of betrayal.' Still clasping her flowers Galina was driven away to spend the next two years in labour camp.

'I will not exchange my conscience for freedom,' she wrote to her father. 'They could not bend you either, nor block out of your soul the love of Christ.'

For Galina, for her harassed parents and fellow-believers, for the prisoners named in this book and the countless unnamed ones, for those who are drugged in mental hospital and yet still find in their souls the love of Christ, for those who are broken and coerced into conformity, Keston College continues its work, challenging the world to grant to its people the right to believe, so that the far horizons of the spirit may open before us. In that wide land we find our freedom and our peace, and dreams may gladden our hearts. Let us give Anatoli Levitin the last word:

> While I was in the concentration camp I had a dream. I was travelling in a boat along the Neva at night-time and there were many stars in the sky. I stepped out of the boat and walked barefoot on the water; the sensation was so realistic that even now I can still recall the coolness of the water under my feet and the thought crossing my mind: 'Surely I'll drown—after all, it must be three times deeper than a man!' Then I reached the bank and someone, invisible in the darkness, stretched out his hand to me.
>
> And I still feel this hand in mine, the hand of my Friend.

[1] *Religion in Communist Lands*, vol. 7, no. 4, winter 1979.

[2] Jean Jenner, 'The Church that will not die', in Gail Lawther (ed.), *Christian Woman*. Herald Publications, 1983.

[3] *RCL*, vol. 4, no. 3, autumn 1976.

[4] Review in RCL, vol. 2, no. 2, March–April 1974.